How to
Transform Your Life With
IMPACT

How to Transform Your Life With IMPACT: Unlock the Best of You
ISBN: 978-17-385225-0-7

This edition published in Great Britain in
2024 by Whalebone Publishing.
First Edition published in 2021
through Amazon Kindle Direct Publishing

Whalebone Publishing is the publishing imprint
tradename for The Book Writers' Resource Ltd

Produced in the UK by The Book Writers' Resource
www.tbwr.co.uk

Copyright © Mark Evans
www.conversationswithimpact.co.uk

Mark Evans has asserted his right under the Copyright, Design and Patents Act 1988 to be identified as the author of this work.

Disclaimer:

This book is sold subject to the condition that it shall not, by way of trade or otherwise, be lent, resold, hired out, or otherwise circulated without the author's prior consent in any form of binding or cover and without a similar condition, including this condition, being imposed on the subsequent publisher.

Illustrations by Dave Johnson.

Dedication

This book is dedicated to the memory of Annie Hersey 1949–2022.

Contents

Introduction ix

I is for IMPACT 1
    The Conversations With Impact Questionnaires 7
    Bridge of Curiosity 19

M is for MEANING 21
    The Meaning Map 32
    The Observing Self activity 47

P is for PATTERNS 53
    The Cliff Edge 56

A is for ACCEPTANCE 85
    Fantasy-Reality Gaps (FRGs) 88
    The Triangle of Possibility 115

C is for CHALLENGE 117
    The 0–10 Challenge 139
    The Stretch Zone 145

T is for TRANSFORMATION 147
    The Ship's Rope 165
    Cave and Continuation Points 170
    Darwinian Tree 183
    The Destination Finder 187

A Final Thought 197

HOW TO TRANSFORM YOUR LIFE WITH
IMPACT
The New Edition

Mark Evans

Introduction

When someone meets me for the first time as a coach or therapist, straight away I want them to feel that I am the right person for them. To achieve this outcome, I need to demonstrate that I can help them to overcome their difficulties and achieve their challenges. I aim for this book to have the same impact on you because I want its title, *How to Transform your Life with IMPACT: Unlock the best of you*, to come true for you.

My book's subject, The IMPACT Model, has been tried and tested over thousands of hours of practise and with thousands of clients (3,500+ at the time of writing). I have seen people use The IMPACT Model to transform their lives from university students to entrepreneurs, business owners, and people in retirement.

The IMPACT Model

The six stages of The IMPACT Model are:

I is for IMPACT: We have all experienced hope and relief when we talk to someone who knows exactly what to say to us. And we have all felt frustration and disappointment when a conversation fails to give us what we need. Persistent difficulties and insurmountable challenges mean our existing conversations are missing the qualities and characteristics we need to get where we want to be. Only 'Conversations With **IMPACT**' can make the difference we are after.

M is for MEANING: Achieving progress depends on us making sense of why things are as they are. Without a clear understanding, we remain a mystery to ourselves, making progress difficult or even impossible. Demystifying—making sense of why things are as they are—makes change happen and helps us find real **MEANING**.

P is for PATTERNS: Positive change depends on us knowing what we are doing a lot of that isn't working and what we are not doing enough of that is. Answering these two questions so we can understand our **PATTERNS** of thought, behaviour, feeling and relating creates a foundation for change.

A is for ACCEPTANCE: Achieving personal growth can stretch, challenge, and reward us. However, if our goals and expectations are unrealistic, we can become demoralised and exhausted. When this happens, our Fantasy-Reality Gaps (FRG) become too large, and **ACCEPTANCE** is how we close them. Acceptance is not resignation but the first stage of transformation.

C is for CHALLENGE: If we had the answer, we would already be the person we want to be, living the life we want to be living. The **CHALLENGE** is to find out what stands in our way and the strategies and resources we need, using The Goldilocks Principle of Challenge: not too little, not too much, but just the right amount.

T is for Transformation: We all want to reach our final destination when our difficulties and challenges have been dealt with and overcome. And yet, if it were that easy, we would all be there by now. An effective approach to **TRANSFORMATION** takes us to our desired destination by mapping out the journey that will get us there.

Whatever prompted you to buy my book, be it a crisis, a sense of stuckness, or a desire to be more and do more in life, the six stages of my Model contain the ideas, knowledge, strategies and techniques to make the difference you are after.

Why have I written this book?

The short answer is this book is another way I can make a difference in people's lives. Conversations change lives; this book is my conversation with you to change yours. New approaches to age-old human problems are like new maps to old territory. Yes, countless people have visited the 'territory' you are on now, but it is constantly evolving, requiring new maps. I believe wholeheartedly that my contribution can add to, rather than duplicate, existing knowledge. If I didn't, I would not have written this book.

Who is this book for?

How to Transform your Life with IMPACT: Unlock the best of you is for anyone facing challenge or adversity, whether personal or professional. Below is a list of issues clients have brought to me that I have written my book to address. Perhaps you recognise one or more of them?

- Enforced change, such as bereavement, redundancy, illness and divorce.
- Chosen life or career change.
- Personal or professional crises.
- Unlocking and realising potential.
- Growing existing strengths and resources.
- Addressing past, present or future concerns.
- Personal and professional development.
- Boosting self-esteem and self-worth.
- Confidence building and assertiveness.
- Coping with identity, role and status change.
- Achieving mental and physical health and wellbeing.
- Improving relationships at home and at work.
- Developing new skills and abilities.
- Acquiring new insights.
- Overcoming problematic lifestyles.
- Being challenged.
- Finding meaning and purpose.

What is this book for?

This is a book for anyone who wants transformation in their lives, like Laura:

> "Hi Mark, it's been a while, which I suppose is a good thing. Just thought I would get in touch to say thanks for all your help. It has completely changed me as a person and completely changed the course of my life. I'm now working in youth and community work and enjoying every minute of it. So out of my comfort zone working with teenagers, but it's great. Anyway, not going to bore you with all the details, but just to say thanks for everything you have done for me."
> Laura

Laura's story is remarkable and culminated, for me at least, in the above message. I worked with Laura for around a year, and her transformation is a testament to what people are capable of with the right information, knowledge and support.

I want The IMPACT Model to be for you what it was for Laura. Firstly, as a manual and guide to take you from where you are to where you want to be, regardless of your start or desired endpoint. Secondly, as a map to help you locate where you are currently on your own journey of transformation, how you got there and the distance left to your desired destination. Finally, I see the Model as a diagnostic tool. Whenever you are stuck or are making progress, you will be able to understand why through reference to its six stages.

How does this book work?

I would love for you to read my book through once and, having gained an appreciation of its contents, read it more systematically, applying The IMPACT Model to your situation. However, if you choose not to do it this way, I have written my book so you can get to work immediately. Also, I am not an academic, and this is not an academic book, so there is no jargon or impenetrable language to bog you down.

The six stages—because they represent concepts that I believe—are non-negotiable for successful transformation, make sense individually and collectively. Feedback from those who have read my book suggests that most apply The IMPACT Model generally to start with, then dip in more selectively. There is, though, no right or wrong way.

Clients often ask me how long their coaching or therapy will take. In my early career, I tried to be helpful by being specific, but I turned out to be a poor clairvoyant. Now I avoid getting into the prediction game. How long will this book take you to complete? How long should you spend on each chapter or activity? My answer – as with coaching and therapy, I would like you to value and commit to yourself by doing what is necessary.

What if you get stuck on one of the Model's six stages or cannot get past a problem or difficulty? Firstly, don't worry; getting stuck is a normal stage of any transformational journey. Being at a loss to know what to do doesn't mean you are failing; it means you don't know how to proceed, which is a different thing entirely. If my IMPACT Model is about anything, it is about the 'How'. So if you get bogged down, persevere and trust in yourself and my book to provide you with the answer you need. Go back through the chapters and activities. Like great stories, they will give you something new each time to free you and get you back on track.

Activities and Tasks

In addition to the six concepts that make up The IMPACT Model, each chapter features a range of activities and tasks to go with them, supplemented by several standalone activities placed in between chapters. I hope they will lift the Model's six concepts off the page and into your life. A happy brain is a busy problem-solving brain, and my activities and tasks will hopefully make your brain a happy one too.

"Whenever I felt stuck, and my stress levels started to rise, I would step onto Mark's Bridge of Curiosity. This activity never failed to help. It detached me from an issue so that I could think more objectively. On my Bridge of Curiosity, I never doubted that a way through existed, and it was where I learned to trust myself again."
Matt.

The role of others

While there is a lot in this book for you individually, there is much that assumes the direct or indirect involvement of other people. Some might play a significant role, while others might be less influential. Either way, others are bound to play a part in your transformation, and I take this into account throughout my book.

For example, the first chapter—I is for IMPACT—addresses your current conversations and whether they are making the difference, you are after. Using my Conversations With IMPACT Questionnaire, you will identify the qualities and characteristics missing from conversations that do not positively impact your life. This information is gold dust. You can use it to transform existing negative conversations into positive ones and, if you decide to talk to someone new, as the starting point for your conversations with them.

There are similar opportunities in the Meaning, Patterns, Acceptance, Challenge and Transformation chapters to think about or involve others as you progress.

Inspiration

Since qualifying as a therapist in 2005, I have worked with some truly unique and inspirational people, and their stories and experiences will crop up throughout the book. I hope they will inspire you as you see how others have made The IMPACT Model work for them. (All identifying details have been changed significantly to maintain confidentiality and anonymity.)

One story is Laura's, which she kindly wrote for this book. Laura takes you through her IMPACT journey and the personal and professional transformation she underwent. I know many readers of the first edition of this book found Laura's story inspiring.

Laura's story

In the two years or so prior to seeing Mark, I had surgery for cancer and developed an intestinal condition. Before that and for more years than I care to remember, I was suffering from what I now know to be Post-Traumatic Stress Disorder due to two traumatic incidents separated by many years. My professional life (I was in the finance world), while successful, was ruining my health due to excessive workload and ridiculous hours. I had avoided therapy because I saw it as an admission of failure, but my best efforts weren't helping, and neither was my antidepressant medication. I felt suicidal, and if I'm being honest, it was only the thought of my husband and children that stopped me from going through with it. My health became so poor that my GP reluctantly had to take my driving licence away. Looking back, losing my ability to drive was the worst thing of all. Gone was my independence.

I is for IMPACT

My husband and GP asked me to reconsider therapy, so I went on a counselling directory and saw Mark's photo and profile. In our first session, he asked me why I had chosen him, and I said that in his photo, he looked kind. I understood the meaning behind the name of his business (Conversations With Impact), so in addition to kindness, I told him he needed to accept me, not judge me, regardless of what I came through the door with each week (I was convinced that even he would hate me for some things I had done). This was the Conversation With Impact I needed as I was surrounded by people who didn't understand what I was going through and who were full of opinions about what I should or should not be doing. Although it took me several months to finally talk about some stuff, Mark's focus on ensuring our conversations gave me what I needed meant I eventually did so. One of the traumatic events in my life took place over thirty years ago, and I had never spoken to anyone about it until Mark—that was how safe our conversations made me feel.

M is for MEANING

I'd always seen myself as a miscalculation on my parent's part—an error. My parents were very young when I was born, which led me to the conclusion I came to. I loved my parents, and they loved me, but once too often, they called me their 'mistake', which did little for my self-image. Mark made a connection between my poor mental health and the dim view I had of myself. The knowledge he shared with me about identity and emotions was a genuine missing piece of my jigsaw. Mark talked a lot about my negative self. He suggested this was who I thought I was and that our job was to get me to see otherwise. I'll admit I found this confusing at first as, if this wasn't who I was, then who was I? As it turned out, I was the one who booked the first therapy session. Mark said turkeys don't vote for Christmas, and negative selves don't book therapy sessions. Understanding that my negative self would not have accessed therapy because therapy is a threat to their dominance put me in contact with the parts of me that I now realise were responsible for my recovery.

P is for PATTERNS

Therapy helped me to identify one particularly destructive pattern. I did not consider myself important and was incapable of doing anything positive for myself. For example, I often worked very late, sometimes into the small hours, and I would wait for a night bus to take me home rather than get a taxi. Despite earning more than enough, I saw such expense as an indulgence I didn't deserve. Consequently, I would arrive home very late, grab a few hours of poor-quality sleep and get up early for work. This pattern of self-neglect was also reflected in my prioritisation of others over myself. The word 'No' was not a part of my vocabulary. No matter who it was or what they wanted, my need for external validation meant I said 'Yes' to every request, even at work. I could only be a 'good' person by helping others, which meant that helping myself would make me 'bad'. My people-pleasing was, I believe, killing me, but until Mark drew my attention to patterns generally and this one, in particular, I had no idea. I still remember the day when I did get a taxi home from work. It was one of the most uncomfortable days of my life, yet so necessary.

A is for ACCEPTANCE

As I said, I would never have considered myself a good person, someone with esteem and worth, but in therapy, I did come to accept myself. Hearing Mark tell me repeatedly that I had worth as a human being eventually sank in. I either accepted what he said, or I had to accuse him of lying. I also accepted that other people and life events had to share some responsibility for who I was and the life I had led. While this had been pointed out, accepting it felt like an excuse. So I stopped rescuing and providing for everyone else. The fear that putting myself first sometimes would result in people abandoning me never materialised. There were some who didn't like being told 'No' and they disappeared from my life, but if that was a bad thing, then why did I feel better? I still gave a lot to my family and friends, but I got the balance right between them and me. I came to accept that fundamentally changing my approach to myself and my life was not a mark of failure but one of achievement.

C is for CHALLENGE

While my overall health was improving, I knew I had to find alternative employment if I was to make a full recovery, which meant changing my career. While not a new realisation, simply thinking about what this challenge would involve caused me to have panic attacks. However, Mark showed me that my panic was not about the goal of changing career but my strategy to achieve it. In other words, I didn't have one. Over time, I developed a realistic, achievable approach to finding my new career that satisfied my need to see progress without causing me the panic of never finding one. That was my worst fear—that I would never find one. Everything depended on this outcome, and I can't tell you the relief I felt when I knew it would be possible. Mark helped me find a level of challenge I could cope with, so I could figure out what I would do next. Luckily I had an extensive network of contacts—a resource Mark suggested I tap into. One of those contacts resulted in a conversation that led me to my new role: working with disadvantaged young adults to help them in their careers.

T is for TRANSFORMATION

At the end of therapy and, as it turned out, coaching as well, I was a fundamentally different person, leading a fundamentally different life. Virtually everything had changed: my career, the number of hours I work, my relationships and my health. The two greatest days were when my intestinal condition was brought under control, and I got my Driving Licence back. I initially chose Mark because he looked kind, but his IMPACT Model showed me where I had been going wrong and what I could do about it. I walk my dogs and enjoy my holidays, and most importantly, my family no longer have to worry about me not being around.

Laura.

I is for IMPACT

All of us have experienced feelings of hope, relief and excitement when a conversation gives us precisely what we need; and all of us have felt despair, disappointment and frustration when a conversation fails to do so. To overcome our difficulties and challenges, we need to have the right conversations with ourselves and others at the right time. When we don't, those difficulties and challenges persist and possibly worsen.

> A conversation can take different forms. It can be interpersonal i.e., involving someone else, and intrapersonal i.e., with ourselves. Increasingly, a conversation can be with someone who sounds human but is 'artificial'. A conversation can occur in various contexts, such as in our heads, homes and workplaces, in the same physical space or virtually where the person we are talking to is somewhere else. I like to think I am conversing with you, the reader, through this book. What defines a Conversation With Impact, however, is not the type but the outcome, and that it makes the difference you are after.

The first stage

The six stages of my IMPACT Model are non-negotiable for successful transformation in who we are, what we do and the life we lead. What is also non-negotiable is the position of I for IMPACT as the first stage. Only by getting this stage right can we make it through the other five because only Conversations With Impact can:

- make the difference we are after: **IMPACT**
- make sense of why things are as they are: **MEANING**
- identify unhelpful, negative patterns and replace them with helpful, positive ones: **PATTERNS**
- find acceptance in who we are, someone with esteem and worth, strengths and potential: **ACCEPTANCE**
- make challenge work for, not against us: **CHALLENGE**
- ensure we complete our journey of transformation: **TRANSFORMATION.**

If it were untrue that we needed Conversations With Impact to flourish in life and build resilience, I would be doing something else right now. There would be no need for coaches, therapists and self-help books because we would already have what we needed to get to where we wanted to be.

In this chapter, which will be a voyage of discovery as you see first-hand why conversations are so influential, I will show you how to:

- have Conversations With Impact by identifying the qualities and characteristics you need
- upgrade conversations, including those you have with yourself (self-talk), which have the potential to become ones that can make the difference you are after
- identify when you need to go outside of your existing support network and find someone new to talk to.

"I thought talking myself down was normal. The idea that I could be nice to myself, not just my team, was alien to me. Over time, I got to experience what it was like to go into meetings with clients or my employees without tearing strips off myself before, during and after. Negative self-talk is exhausting, and as I discovered, directly impacted my performance, which was not something I could afford running a large business. Changing how I talk to myself has made a huge difference."
Sue

What is a Conversation With Impact?

A Conversation With Impact is one we have with ourselves or others that contains what we need to make the difference we are after. It demonstrates that it is different by including the qualities and characteristics missing from our existing conversations, such as trust, positivity and helpful ideas. And it is this difference that creates the IMPACT because it gives us the experience of a conversation that can resolve the problems we face or help us achieve the goals we have set for ourselves. In my work, I never underestimate the 'impact' this has. When I do my job well and give someone a Conversation With Impact, I see them visibly change in front of me as the reality hits them that I can and will help.

A Conversation With Impact always leaves us with more than what we started with, fundamentally changing who we are and what we know because it is based on an effective relationship with ourselves or others that brings new:

- ideas and perspectives
- goals and objectives
- techniques and strategies
- information and knowledge.

A Conversation With Impact positively influences our other conversations. It removes the pressure from existing conversations to make the difference we are after, often to the relief of those closest to us; changes how we talk to ourselves and others and what we talk about; and enables us to distinguish between conversations that are worth continuing and those that are not. Finding someone who can give us a Conversation With Impact, or be able to do so for ourselves, means we no longer waste valuable time and energy engaging in conversations that take us further from where we want or need to be.

> "I would batter myself with self-criticism. Give myself a daily diet of self-sabotage, 'That wasn't good enough,' or, 'Really? That's it? That's all you have to offer?' I now understand why I did this and how not to."
> Graham

I IS FOR IMPACT

QUESTIONNAIRE

The Conversations With Impact Questionnaires

Below are my Conversations With Impact Questionnaires, which I designed to help people identify what they need from a conversation to make the difference they are after. The Questionnaire on this page addresses your conversations with others, and the one on page 8 tackles your conversations with yourself. Both include what I consider to be the essential qualities and characteristics of a Conversation With Impact—completing the Questionnaires will enable you to build a detailed picture of your existing conversations and what you can do to improve them.

To get started, I will first ask you to familiarise yourself with the Questionnaires and then complete the activity underneath, which includes how to score each quality and characteristic.

Statement	Score	Statement	Score
I trust the person		They understand me and what I need from them	
I feel respected by them		They have the ideas, knowledge and skills I need	
They do not judge me and accept me for who I am		They believe in me and my potential for change	
Our conversations follow my agenda, not theirs		I feel challenged by them in a good way	
They give me the time I need		I feel they genuinely listen to me	

Statement	Score	Statement	Score
They respect my need for confidentiality		They are truly interested in me	
I can say what I really want to them		They help me set clear, realistic goals and strategies	
They help me make sense of my situation		My conversations with them make a difference	
They keep me focused		They keep me accountable	
They help me find solutions to my problems		They have the X-Factor	

Statement	Score	Statement	Score
I trust myself		I understand myself and what I need from myself	
I respect myself		I have the ideas, knowledge and skills I need	
I do not judge myself, and I accept myself for who I am		I believe in myself and my potential for change	
My self-talk follows my, not others', agendas		I challenge myself in a good way	
I give myself the time I need		I genuinely listen to myself	

Statement	Score	Statement	Score
I respect my confidentiality and do not overshare		I am truly interested in myself	
I can say what I really want to myself		I set myself clear, realistic goals and strategies	
I can make sense of my situation		My conversations with myself (my self-talk) make a difference	
I can keep myself focused		I can keep myself accountable	
I can find solutions to my problems		I have the X-Factor	

Existing conversations

What conversations should you include? The list below gives some suggestions but select those relevant to your issues. In other words, if you enter a daily conversation with the owner of your local shop, this might be one to leave out. Conversations to consider are those with:

- yourself (necessary)
- partners
- friends
- family
- acquaintances
- colleagues
- bosses
- professionals, such as coaches, therapists or mentors

- social and cultural representatives, such as teachers, community and spiritual figures
- artificial interfaces, such as apps and other technologies.

Both Questionnaires work in the same way. Start by listing your relevant conversations. Then, choose a number between 1 and 7 that reflects the degree to which the conversation possesses each quality and characteristic (1=none, 7=all that you need). When scoring your conversations, consider the importance of each quality or characteristic to you. If one is unimportant to you i.e., it makes no difference one way or the other, give it a 7. For those that are important to you, score them appropriately. Remember to keep a copy of your completed questionnaires. You will need them.

The number of completed questionnaires should equal the number of conversations you selected initially.

What did you discover?

It is important to remember there are no right or wrong combinations of qualities or characteristics, which means there are no right or wrong scores. However, in my experience:

- conversations with mostly low scores (3 or below) tend to make things worse
- conversations with mostly medium scores (4 or 5) tend to make little or no difference
- conversations with mostly high scores (6 or 7) tend to make a significant, positive difference.

Looking at your scores, what do they say about your existing conversations? How might they explain the existence and persistence of your difficulties or lack of progress towards key goals and objectives? Or alternatively, how might they clarify the opposite, your consistent ability to achieve personal and professional transformation?

Conversations with yourself

Please do not neglect your conversations with yourself, as they will be the one constant as you commit to transforming yourself. Aim for your self-talk to become as important, influential and pivotal as any other conversation you have. When we don't have anyone else to talk to, being able to give ourselves a Conversation With Impact is essential, and even when we have great support around us, it is rarely enough by itself.

> "I learnt what an effective conversation was and that those I was giving myself were very far from being effective. Now my conversations with myself are effective. I have become my own life coach."
> Katherine

Looking at the questionnaire for conversations with yourself and the scores you allocated for each quality and characteristic, consider the following:

- what do you need to find more of?
- what do you need to maintain?
- what would make them Conversations with Impact?

If you have given yourself mostly low or mostly low-to-medium scores, indicating your self-talk is harmful, there are usually good reasons for this, such as low self-esteem, perfectionism or the effect of an unhappy or toxic relationship. If this is what you suspect or discover, however hard it is to accept, trust the whole book to show you what you can do to improve your situation.

If you have given yourself mainly medium scores, ask yourself how you can get them higher. Or, if your scores are predominantly high, what can you do to maintain them?

Conversations with others:
Same people, improved conversations?

Achieving a Conversation With Impact does not necessarily mean changing who you are talking to. If you have identified a conversation that isn't having the desired impact, but has the potential to do so, look at its scores. Which qualities and characteristics, if increased, would turn this conversation into a Conversation With Impact? Share the findings of your questionnaire with the person concerned. They are clearly important to you in some way, and their involvement allows you both to focus on what you need. All I would say is to think carefully about approaching anyone in this situation and how you will do so. Even though you might value their conversations, are they someone you can talk to about this or not? If they are and they agree to try and give you what you need, then great. Agree with them on the importance of ongoing assessment of your updated conversations to ensure they become and remain Conversations With Impact. If you decide not to ask them, that's ok. You can continue to benefit from the relationship, knowing that you will need to find someone else.

Important people, low scores?

What if low scores apply to someone significant to you in some way, someone you have to talk to? As a coach and therapist, I am acutely aware that we can't always change our partner or boss, even if we want to. When it comes to such people and our conversations with them, you have to be kind to yourself, even selfish (in a good way), by asking if:

- you have the ability or inclination to talk to them about what you need
- they are someone who will be receptive to changing how they speak to you.

If you decide not to try, please back yourself in making this decision. Feeling guilty, deceitful or ashamed can be easy because you lack the courage. Please don't. If you have issues that this person can't or won't help you with, you have every right to seek someone who can and will.

A final thought. If the outcome of finding someone else who can give you a Conversation With Impact is increased self-confidence, this presents you with an interesting dilemma. Do you return to this 'important' person and ask for an improved conversation, assuming they are still in your life? If you do because the decision is more about marking your progress than whether they agree to change how they talk to you, I'd say go for it. If they are amenable, how amazing would that be? But if they aren't, you are now in a position to decide whether this person needs to remain a part of your life. Imagine how amazing that would be, a win-win situation.

> "My husband used to criticise me for lacking ambition. My attempts to get him to understand that I just had different ambitions to him, were always rejected. Completing the questionnaire showed me what my husband wasn't giving me: unconditional support. I showed him the questionnaire I did for our conversations. He apologised and decided to support me."
> Nina

Need someone new to talk to?

If completing my Questionnaires makes it clear you need someone new to talk to, here are some points to consider. Whoever you find, explain that you are talking to them because your existing conversations are not making the difference you are after. Show them your questionnaires and scores, being specific about the qualities and characteristics you are looking for. If they can provide them, then great, but if they can't, no hard feelings. Finding someone who can give you a Conversation With Impact is important, and what is important is worth taking time for.

Remember, this book is about your transformation into the person you want to be, living the life you want to be living, which are outcomes only a Conversation With Impact can deliver.

What to talk about?

Whether you decide to improve an existing conversation or find someone new to talk to, the next step is determining what to speak to them about, which gives me a chance to introduce the following list of areas that will feature throughout this book. These areas are where we will find both the causes of our difficulties, their solutions and opportunities for our transformation.

- Yourself: identity, role and status; self-esteem and self-worth.
- Home and family life.
- Relationships – personal and professional.
- Work, career and professional development.
- Health and wellbeing.
- Financial.
- Lifestyle.
- Social.
- Cultural.
- Environmental.

To get you started, think about the areas you want my book to help you with. Using a 0–10 scale, where 0 = an area in great shape and 10 = an area in very poor shape, allocate numbers that capture how you currently feel about each area. As a general rule:

- Areas scored 7 or above require immediate attention
- Areas scored 5 or 6 require attention soon
- Areas scored 4 or below can be nurtured or even left alone

This activity aims to be diagnostic. Looking at your scores, what do they suggest you should be talking about and to whom? For example, if your professional transformation is a priority, can you turn to your existing support network, or do you need to find someone new such as a Careers Coach? Or, if your past is the most pressing concern because of trauma, do you need someone experienced in this field? Remember, only Conversations with Impact can make the difference you are after. There is no point in choosing someone who can't give you what you need.

How to have a Conversation With Impact

At a practical level, the 'how' can happen as soon as you act on your questionnaires' outcomes, e.g., by changing how you talk to yourself, asking a partner for an improved conversation or finding a professional to work with. Once started, focus on the qualities and characteristics you need from these conversations, assessing their impact by regularly completing new questionnaires. If you are not moving forwards, new questionnaires will enable you to find out what is missing and will explain your lack of progress, and if you are progressing, they will show you why. If it becomes clear that your conversations are not having the desired impact, consider how you and the people you are talking to can get back on track by finding more of the qualities and characteristics you need. And if it doesn't prove possible? Be kind to yourself and find someone new to talk to.

At an emotional level, assessing what you are and are not capable of when it comes to having Conversations With Impact will be essential. If you feel confident, then there is no stopping you. However, if you feel unconfident, whoever you speak to must make you feel safe. Talk to a professional like a life coach or therapist if in doubt.* Work with them until you can ask for a Conversation With Impact from anyone.

Whatever your starting point, commit to having Conversations With Impact.

---

* For information on the differences between life coaching and therapy, the following organisations have lots of helpful information: www.counselling-directory.org.uk and www.lifecoach-directory.org.uk.

What stops people from having a Conversation With Impact?

There are several reasons. Often people don't know that their conversations are the issue in the first place. Or if they have some idea, they lack sufficient understanding of what is missing, or have no way of finding out and consequently can't ask for what they need. Another explanation is that the people they are talking to don't know how to give them the conversation they need or, worse, do know but don't want to.

Stigma, shame, or embarrassment can prevent people from accessing services like therapy, as can the fear of what conversations with professionals might be like.

The more concerning reason is when someone stops themselves from asking for a Conversation With Impact. 'What if my partner leaves me?' 'What if my boss sacks me?' Many of us will have found ourselves in this position due to fear or a lack of confidence, knowing we cannot deal with the consequences of rejection or being ignored. As I said above, in situations like these, the focus must be on addressing what is stopping someone. We all need to reach the stage where we can ask for a Conversation With Impact from anyone we trust to help us.

Summary of chapter one

- Persistent difficulties and challenges result from conversations that are missing important qualities and characteristics, which means they can never make the difference we are after.
- Conversations With Impact become possible when we incorporate into new conversations the qualities and characteristics missing from our existing ones.
- The Conversations With Impact Questionnaires can change how you talk to yourself and the people you already know and help you decide if you need someone new to talk to.

- Conversations With Impact are critical for our personal and professional transformation, and we must remove any barriers that prevent us from having them.

"I attended a workshop run by Mark and was struck by the idea that I had never thought about whether my conversations were helpful or not. The biggest change has been in my relationship with my 18-year-old son. He told me he found it difficult to open up to me about his anxiety. He completed a Questionnaire for our conversations and it showed me that I try to fix things and take control of his life, whereas what he needed from me was to listen and ask how I can support him."
Sarah

THE BRIDGE OF CURIOSITY

Bridge of Curiosity

Where you are now is not where you want to be. Where you want to be is somewhere else, but your difficulty is you don't know where that somewhere else is or how to get there. You know you have to get to where you want to be because staying where you are isn't an option. As you ponder your predicament, a bridge appears in front of you. While you can't see over to the other side, you have a sixth sense that stepping onto it is the right thing to do. You notice the bridge is made of stone and etched into one of the stones on the right-hand side is what you assume to be its name, 'The Bridge of Curiosity'. And then you notice that the bridge is etched with other writings, all in the form of questions.

'Why do you need to get to the other side?'

'What do you not have or know that will get you to the other side?'

'Who can show you how to get across?'

'Who will you be over the other side?'

The more you look, the more questions you see. And the more you see, the more curious you become. And the more curious you become, the more the bridge appears ahead. "Now that is curious," you say to yourself.

An idea pops into your head. You look away from the questions and stop being curious. "Yes," you say, "I knew it!" For up ahead, the bridge seems to disappear into nothingness. You have no choice. Only curiosity will get you over to the other side and where you want to be. And so you let your curiosity get to work, helped along by the questions carved into the bridge. Then, just as suddenly as the first side of the Bridge of Curiosity appeared, so does the other side. Looking straight ahead, you see a beautiful landscape opening up in front of you. Your attention is drawn to a sign that removes any doubt about what you are seeing. It says, 'Where you want to be.' As you reach the end of the bridge, you notice a hammer and chisel resting against its righthand side. Picking them up, you chisel a question of your own into the stone. Then you step off.

MARK EVANS

M is for MEANING

"As silly as it sounds, I found myself shouting at my dogs. Whenever it was walkies they would go nuts with excitement—because they're dogs. But this would really, really get me angry. I mean I would go ballistic. It was only when my wife admitted that I was scaring her that I did something about it. What I came to realise was that I needed life to be just so, for people, my dogs and life to do as they're told, to toe the line. And then the penny dropped. My anger was linked to control. I am not joking when I say my whole life suddenly made sense."
Duncan

The need for meaning brings two types of people together: those in need of meaning and those who help them find it, of which my professions—coaching and therapy—are two. Meaning is a stage of my IMPACT Model because, in its various forms, it can make the difference between paralysis and progress in life. In this chapter, I consider meaning in the following way: to make sense of why things are as they are. I realise there is a great deal more to the topic of meaning, such as meaning something to others or leading a meaningful life, but these are addressed more generally by the whole book.

Why things are as they are

Often what motivates someone to work with someone like me or to pick up a book like this is that they cannot understand—make sense of—why things are as they are. They might know they are stuck or in trouble, but the 'why' is shrouded in mystery. So, what do I mean by 'things'? I mean anything that someone has become aware of that is, to varying degrees of severity, problematic for them. Examples I come across in my work include:

- intrusive thoughts or unpleasant physical symptoms
- harmful or destructive behaviours, such as obsessions, compulsions and addictions
- difficult emotions, such as stress, anxiety, depression or anger
- low self-esteem and self-worth, low self-confidence
- issues with identity and sexuality
- social and cultural issues that limit who someone is or what they can do
- relationship problems like separation and divorce
- personal and professional stuckness or challenge
- lacking meaning and purpose, or direction in life
- combinations of the above.

Making sense of

I see 'making sense of' as the active process by which someone seeks to explain the existence in their lives of phenomena, like those in the list above, or the absence of something they expect or want to have. Sense-making can be a solo effort, for example, when someone is alone with their thoughts or a collective endeavour when two or more people try to work things out. And it can draw on a range of information, knowledge and resources, such as newspapers and magazines, podcasts, film and television, and the internet.

Human beings are a sense-making species, an ability upon which our thriving and surviving depends. An inability to make sense of our experiences makes it hard to articulate what we are going through to ourselves and others. How many of us, when asked by a partner or friend, "What's wrong? What's the matter?" have replied, "I don't know." While we don't always need an exact explanation, even if one can be extremely helpful, we do need the ability to make enough sense of our difficulties and challenges, if we are to progress in life.

> "My mental health was shocking throughout my teens. Working through a timeline of my life with Mark, when I reached 13 years old, I remembered that someone tried to sexually assault me on a family holiday. I was fine before I was 13. No one had ever linked my mental health to that event even though they knew about it. Years of GP visits and therapy and all I needed was for someone to make sense of that experience for me."
> Lucy

An emotional mystery tour

An inability to make sense of why things are as they are, generates 'difficult' emotions like stress and anxiety. Emotions like these are how our mind/body systems complain when they observe that we don't appear to know what is going on with our lives at times when we really need to. Being in a state of ignorance sets in motion a vicious cycle:

- stress and anxiety caused by our difficulties
- stress and anxiety caused by our inability to make sense of them
- stress and anxiety caused by the resultant deterioration in the quality of our lives.

Some mystery tours are fun; this one isn't, especially if it goes on too long. Unfortunately, our hardwired need to make sense of our situation—to 'demystify'—means we are destined to remain on our emotional mystery tour until we do.

Looking in the wrong place

Understandably, we can find ourselves in an energy-sapping focus on what we do know, namely, the symptoms and effects of our difficulties. These come in various forms and are often the catalyst for people to act or others to comment. Examples include:

- physical symptoms such as chest pain, stomach issues and headaches
- negative, intrusive thoughts
- difficult emotional states such as stress, anxiety, depression and anger
- problematic behaviours such as avoidance, procrastination or perfectionism
- unhealthy lifestyles such as alcohol dependency, drug use and overeating
- relationship problems such as irritability, conflict
- professional issues such as work-related stress.

It is hard not to pay attention to the above symptoms and effects, especially as they can be distressing and disruptive, but doing so will only prove effective if we can make sense of them. If we can't, we and anyone else trying to support us are looking in the wrong place. How do we know we are looking in the wrong place? Because our symptoms and effects persist and usually worsen.

Looking in the right place

A few years ago, when I was a student coach and therapist in Higher Education, I worked with a severely depressed student who I shall call Tim. In the final year of an accountancy degree, Tim was very concerned that his poor mental health would make it hard for him to graduate. Tim cut a forlorn figure, his head hung low and his eyes fixed firmly on the floor.

It quickly emerged that his depression was a mystery to him, and despite some initial exploration, it remained this way for both of us. However, something didn't add up for me. There, sitting opposite me, was an accountancy student wearing a Sex Pistols T-shirt, a leather jacket, skinny black jeans and sporting a hairstyle like Johnny Rotten. I had worked with many accountancy students, and he looked like none of them. Leaning forward to gain eye contact with Tim, I asked, "Why are you studying accountancy?"

He looked up and replied, "I don't know."

"If you don't mind me saying," I continued, "you don't look like a typical accountancy student."

"I hate it," he said. "I'm only here because of my family—to make them proud."

I asked him what he would rather be doing. "Playing in my band back in Hartlepool with my mates. We're pretty good and want to give ourselves a chance."

And there it was: meaning.

"Is that why I'm depressed?" he asked.

"Yes, I think it probably is," I replied.

I saw Tim for a further two sessions. He was transformed. That summer, I received an email from him.

"Hi Mark, thought you would like to know. I graduated with a 2:1 and am midway through a tour with my band. My family are truly proud of me. I want you to know the difference you made in helping me make sense of my depression. It released something, and I will never forget that feeling." Tim

Tim spent three years (the duration of his course) looking in the wrong place. GP visits, different antidepressant medications, conversations with family and friends, and practical help from his university tutors—none of which clarified anything. So, how do we know where the right place to look is? Let your emotions guide you.

Finding the right place: emotions as messages

I have long subscribed to the idea that emotions are messages, a form of communication containing vital information designed to help us to thrive and survive. So when it comes to making sense of why things are as they are and finding the right place to look for answers, emotions are a great guide. In fact, I would suggest that this is one of their primary functions.

> There are different ways of defining thriving and surviving, but I see it as the ability to maximise the good times and be resilient through the tough ones. Thriving and surviving is the only show in town for all living things, including humans; it is the optimal state we must achieve, maintain or return to. Our task is to understand what thriving and surviving means for us at different stages of our lives and how to achieve it.

As a practitioner, I encourage my clients to see emotions like any other important messages: make sure they are received, made sense of and responded to. Over the following few pages, I will show you how to make this powerful idea work for you.

Applying the emotions as messages concept, 'difficult' emotions, such as stress, anxiety, depression, and anger, are messages indicating that our thriving and surviving are being hampered or threatened in some way. The opposite is conveyed by 'positive' emotions, such as joy, contentment and serenity.

Introducing your Emotional Self

If emotions are messages, then who is the sender? Let me introduce you to your Emotional Self. I have worked with thousands of clients in my career, and this has proven to be one of my most effective concepts. People quickly grasp the idea of a message-sending Emotional Self because sending and receiving messages is a normal part of our lives. When we feel an emotion, we are being invited into a dialogue with our Emotional Selves, which is always about the same thing: the current state of our thriving and surviving. Once this is understood, we can become active participants in some of the most significant conversations we will ever have.

Regardless of which emotional state we are in at any one time, it is vital to understand that our Emotional Selves are always trying to be helpful. After all, their job is to help us achieve the optimal state of thriving and surviving. With positive emotions, it is easy to think of 'helpful' Emotional Selves, but with difficult emotions, like those, I have mentioned, how is this being helpful? I accept this is a tough sell. You won't need me to tell you about the adverse effects that emotional states like depression can have on our lives. They remind us that something is wrong while simultaneously hindering our ability to do anything about it. Again, how is that being helpful?

When it comes to difficult emotions, I am encouraging you to look beyond their symptoms and effects and to their purpose of helping us to thrive and survive. As humans, we do not experience these emotions for no reason; there will be an explanation, and in most cases, something can be done to help those experiencing them. Therefore, we must befriend our Emotional Selves. Yes, they might deliver really helpful messages in really unhelpful ways, but an Emotional Self that feels listened to and understood will be kind to us in return.

There are two parts to our emotional messages that our Emotional Selves want us to know. The first part is about the causes of our emotions, most importantly our difficulties; the second is about responses. As you will see, we must also understand whether causes and responses are internal or external to us—or both.

Causes

In chapter one, in the section, 'What to talk about?' (page 13 and 14), I suggested that the areas below *'...are where we will find both the causes of our difficulties, their solutions and opportunities for our transformation'*:

- yourself: identity, role and status; self-esteem and self-worth
- home and family life
- relationships – personal and professional
- work, career and professional development
- health and wellbeing
- financial
- lifestyle
- social
- cultural
- environment.

In the 21st Century, thriving and surviving means getting these areas in the best shape possible as often and for as long as possible. So when, as happens to all of us, we struggle in one or more of these areas, our Emotional Selves will have something to say.

When they send the first part of their message about the causes of our difficulties, they are asking us two things: identify the problematic area(s) and establish whether it is internal or external to us.

Examples of internal causes of difficult emotions include:

- low self-esteem

Low self-esteem makes thriving and surviving hard because of its characteristic self-critical thoughts and self-defeating behaviours. The message from someone's Emotional Self is, "Please boost your self-esteem and positively change how you think and behave."

- Trauma

In its many forms, trauma can severely undermine our thriving and surviving. The message from someone's Emotional Self is,

"Please resolve your trauma so you can function effectively and live a normal life."

Examples of external causes of difficult emotions include:

- insecure employment

   Feeling insecure at work can undermine our sense of security and need for control. The message from someone's Emotional Self is, "Please change your professional circumstances until you feel secure and back in control."

- Unsafe environment

   Unsafe environments, whether at home, in our community or at work, can similarly destabilise us. The message from someone's Emotional Self is, "Change or leave your current environment until you feel secure and back in control."

This first part of our emotional messages is plain and simple:

- difficult emotions: something is wrong, please do something about it
- positive emotions: something is right, continue what you are doing

Responses

The second part of the message indicates how near or far our Emotional Selves think we are from thriving and surviving and whether it likes our responses. The further away they believe we are, the more intense and difficult the emotion; the closer we are, the more intense and positive the emotion.

Examples of internal responses i.e., solutions and opportunities for our transformation, include:

- boosting self-esteem
- improving our health and wellbeing.

Examples of external responses include:

- changing jobs or career
- ending an unhappy relationship.

This second part of our emotional message is, you guessed it, also plain and simple:

- difficult emotions: your response isn't working; please address why
- positive emotions: your response is working; please continue implementing it.

Emotional Selves take their roles very seriously and carry them out at any cost because our thriving and surviving is so critical. If there is one thing our Emotional Selves hate more than anything, it is being ignored. Ignoring our Emotional Selves doesn't make them go away with an indifferent shrug of the shoulders. Far from it, in fact. When we ignore them, they assume we don't know our thriving and surviving are at stake, which sets their alarm bells ringing. Being ignored makes our Emotional Selves dig their heels in because what they want and are determined to get—especially when we are struggling in life—is us into dialogue with them.

If you want to appreciate fully how determined our Emotional Selves can get, you only need to look at the extreme end of the emotional spectrum. The following are all ways Emotional Selves expresses its concern that our thriving and surviving is at the point of collapse: severe stress, panic attacks, crushing depression, explosive anger.

Knocking loudly at your front door

To get across to people how committed Emotional Selves are, I take them through my 'Knocking loudly at your front door' analogy.

Imagine one day you are sitting at home when there is a knock at the door. You check the time, decide that it can't be someone important, and choose to ignore whoever it is. There is another knock, slightly louder this time, but your response is the same. A little game ensues for the next few minutes: they knock, and you ignore. Thoughts about who the knocker might be come and go in your imagination. A double-glazing salesman, perhaps. Whoever it is, their knocking has become a great deal louder and very annoying. You move to a room at the back of your house, but there is no escape. By now, the hammering on your front door has reached a crescendo, and it occurs to you that you could have made a big mistake. Why did you assume it was someone of insignificance? Someone that determined, you think to yourself, could have critical news for me—an accident, or worse. A jolt of electricity shoots through your body. Then a tremendous crash. You run to your front door, which is now lying on its side in your hallway, no longer attached to its frame. Standing in the entranceway is someone who looks vaguely familiar.

"What the hell?" you shout, surveying the damage. "Who are you? What do you want?"

"I'm your Emotional Self," comes the reply, "and don't ever ignore me again."

A failure to communicate

The trouble is that our Emotional Selves don't communicate effectively with us. They don't talk to us, text, email or DM. All they have at their disposal is an array of emotions that they utilise with varying degrees of intensity depending on whether they are getting their message through. Our Emotional Selves wholly rely on us knowing they exist and their raison d'etre to support our thriving and surviving. They need us to be great receivers, translators and responders of their emotional messages, and until we are, we're in trouble. Hence why I designed my IMPACT Model and have written this book.

The Meaning Map

"I knew I was stressed, but I didn't know why. Mark took me through The Meaning Map, and in about five minutes, the mystery of my stress was solved. Not only that. The Map exercise turned what I thought was going on its head. I thought my life as a whole was causing my stress, whereas the Map revealed that only one or two areas were to blame. This was unexpected but in a good way, like changing a single fuse rather than rewiring your entire house."
John

Now that you know you have an Emotional Self and it is in 24/7 communication with you about the state of your thriving and surviving, the next step is to make sense of what they are saying to you, which my Meaning Map activity will help you to achieve. It will get you into an effective dialogue with your Emotional Self.

In the tables below are the areas you now know you need to get right in life to thrive and survive, where you will find the causes of your difficulties and what you will need responses for. In a nutshell, the contents of this table are all your Emotional Self cares about. Step one involves assessing the current state of your areas, and step two consists of evaluating your responses.

Step One

Using a 0–10 scale (0 = an area in great shape, 10 = an area in very poor shape), choose numbers that 'map out' how you currently feel about each area. As a general rule:

- scores of 7 or more indicate areas in poor or very poor shape that your Emotional Self will be very concerned about.
- Scores of 5 or 6 indicate areas in moderately poor shape that your Emotional Self will be reasonably concerned about.

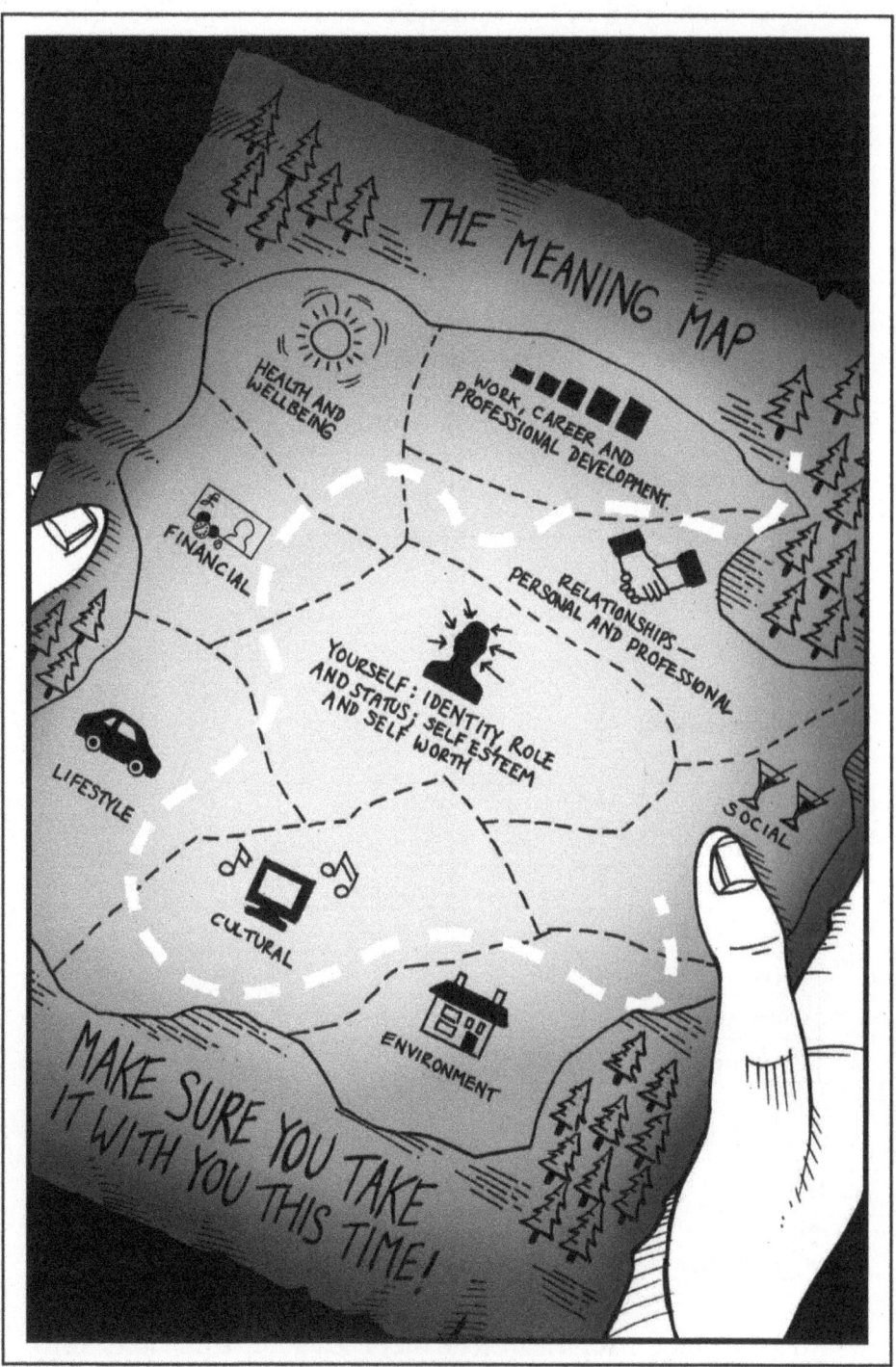

THE MEANING MAP

- Scores of 4 or below indicate areas in good to very good shape that your Emotional Self will be *happy-to-very-happy* about.

The Meaning Map: causes		
Area	**Score**	**Positive, neither good nor bad, negative**
Yourself: identity, role and status; self-esteem and self-worth		
Home and family life		
Relationships – personal and professional		
Work, career and professional development		
Health and wellbeing		
Financial		
Lifestyle		
Social		
Cultural		
Environment		

What did you discover? Thinking about the emotions you are experiencing on a regular or even permanent basis, which you now know are messages, is your Emotional Self happy with the state of your thriving and surviving or are they concerned? If they are concerned, which areas do they think are the primary causes of your difficulties? Which areas do they need positive responses for?

Step two

Using the same 0–10 scale, now choose numbers that reflect the state of your responses i.e., the solutions to your difficulties. As a general rule:

- scores of 7 or more indicate areas which your responses are wholly inadequate for, causing your Emotional Self great concern.
- Scores of 5 or 6 indicate areas which your responses will neither improve nor worsen, causing your Emotional Self moderate concern.
- Scores of 4 or below indicate areas which your responses will improve to a significant or very significant degree, causing your Emotional Self to feel greatly reassured.

The Meaning Map: responses		
Area	Score	Positive, neither good nor bad, negative
Yourself: identity, role and status; self-esteem and self-worth		
Home and family life		
Relationships – personal and professional		
Work, career and professional development		
Health and wellbeing		
Financial		

The Meaning Map: responses		
Area	**Score**	**Positive, neither good nor bad, negative**
Lifestyle		
Social		
Cultural		
Environment		

What did you discover? Thinking about the emotions you are experiencing on a regular or even permanent basis, which you now know are messages, is your Emotional Self happy with your responses or not? Where do they need to see improvement and proactivity if they are concerned?

If you get stuck, use my client Harry's completed version below to help (I have combined his two tables into one). Note that while Harry's 'causes and responses' scores are the same, they don't have to be. If yours are different, that's fine.

The Meaning Map: causes and responses		
Area	**Score**	**Positive, neither good nor bad, negative**
Yourself: identity, role and status; self-esteem and self-worth	7 (C), 7 (R)	Causes: loss of identity is a big issue. I'm a husband, father, business owner, son and brother, but not Harry. I need to be Harry again. Responses: I need to start doing things for myself, starting with talking to my partner and kids about why this is important and why I need their support.

The Meaning Map: causes and responses		
Home and family life	7, 7	Causes: being there for everyone else and neglecting myself is unsustainable. I don't want to become selfish, but I do want a better balance between being there for others and being there for myself. Responses: as above for identity. I need to start the conversation.
Relationships – personal and professional	3, 3	Nothing wrong other than not seeing my friends as often as I'd like to, but this will change as I work on myself, home and family life.
Work, career and professional development	4, 4	Causes: generally, this is a good area for me, but I know that my loss of identity impacts me to a degree. I see colleagues who appear to really know who they are, and I feel envious of them. Responses: working on myself will help me nudge this number still lower.
Health and wellbeing	5, 5	Causes: Generally ok, as we lead pretty full lives, but I fall down on the exercise and eating. Responses: as for health and wellbeing.
Financial	2, 2	All good. More money always welcome!

The Meaning Map: causes and responses		
Lifestyle	5, 5	Causes: Generally ok, as we lead pretty full lives, but I fall down on the exercise and eating. Responses: as for health and wellbeing.
Social	2, 2	All good. Feel connected locally and at work. Watching Nottingham Forest every week is non-negotiable (even if stressful at times!)
Cultural	2, 2	All good. I love volunteering for Age Concern. I know that I make a difference and add something to my community.
Environment	2, 2	All good.

Delivered, translated and responded to

The Meaning Map activity aims to get you into effective and regular communication with your Emotional Self. We want them to know you will be:

- demonstrating a serious commitment to improving areas scored 7 or more
- focusing on improving areas scored 5 or 6
- maintaining or even strengthening areas scored 4 or below.

Don't worry too much at this stage if you don't know your problem areas or your responses because discovering them is the purpose of the whole book and IMPACT Model. For now, focus on deepening your relationship with your Emotional Self. Let them know you understand them and what they want for you: to thrive and survive.

Emotions as messages: past, present and future

Another way we can make sense of why things are as they are is to think about our emotional messages from a time perspective. Human beings exist in time, and who we are, what we do and the life we lead are all characterised by it. Indeed, we can think of our mind/body systems as time machines operating simultaneously in our past, present and future.

Given the importance of time, it will be no surprise that our Emotional Selves keep a keen eye on it. Our thriving and surviving depends on a harmonious relationship between our past, present and future. If we enjoy consistent, positive emotional states, this is a sign that our Emotional Selves are happy with how we are aligning our past, present and future. Alignment means carrying forth what has worked from our past and letting go of what hasn't; making the best of our present; and having positive, realistic goals and strategies for our future. The opposite, therefore, is true. Consistent negative emotional states mean our Emotional Selves are unhappy regarding our past, present and future alignment.

While the past, present and future will all be relevant, we need to know the relative influence of each of them to make sense of why things are as they are. Sometimes, our past will be dominant, and at other times, our present or future. Focusing solely on the future, for example, when it is evident that problems lie in the past, will get us nowhere fast. To repeat: alignment and progress means knowing the relative influence of our past, present and future.

> "Even at primary school, I knew that I would be the one who wouldn't go to university. From a young age, I saw myself as stupid and incapable of doing well. My past had dictated my entire life. With this understanding, I changed my present view of myself. I am now a trainee accountant with a future to look

forward to. Not bad for someone who left school and college with nothing. I look back at my young self with compassion and empathy, knowing they got themselves wrong."
Faisal

However, if we can only partially, not wholly disentangle our past, present and future, this isn't necessarily a problem. The simultaneous operation across these three areas of time by our mind/body systems means that changes made in one area can produce changes in the others. Faisal's moving testimony is an example of how someone working mainly in the present—going to university and building a career—improved their past and future, thus aligning all three. In any case, our Emotional Selves will let us know whether we are working in the right areas. If we are, their emotional messages will be positive; if we aren't, they will be less so. As a coach and therapist, I take my lead from a client's emotional messages: if they are negative, I know the focus isn't right; if they are positive, I know it is.

The Meaning Map: adding the past, present and future

As you can see, The Meaning Map now comes with a past, present and future column. For each area, fill in the information from both stages of your first Meaning Map, and then add past, present or future or combinations of, as appropriate.

The Meaning Map			
Area	Score	Positive, neither good nor bad, negative	Past, present or future
Yourself: identity, role and status; self-esteem and self-worth			

The Meaning Map			
Home and family life			
Relationships – personal and professional			
Work, career and professional development			
Health and wellbeing			
Financial			
Lifestyle			
Social			
Cultural			
Environment			

A coherent narrative

When it comes to making sense of why things are as they are, a coherent narrative for our lives that captures our past, present and future can be highly beneficial, as having one can reduce the guesswork involved as we seek to make sense of our experiences. Lacking a coherent narrative, like any other hindrance to finding meaning, leaves us to work things out from what we do know: the symptoms and effects of our difficulties (see the list on Page 24), which, as I have suggested, can be diagnostically unreliable.

A coherent narrative typically consists of specific details, plus broader themes, such as:

- memories
- the key people in our lives and their influence on us

- significant events and happenings
- formative periods and stages, such as those belonging to our early years, teens and adulthood
- general life patterns, such as achievements and successes, positive and negative relationships, good or poor health and wellbeing, and self-esteem and self-worth.

All of the above can make a valuable contribution. However, in my experience, there isn't a perfect mix. In other words, avoid getting caught up, as some people do, in a futile search for the one memory or event that explains 'everything' as it might not exist.

Vicki came to see me for severe anxiety, the trigger for which was being alone. So bad had the issue become that she would wait in a local café for her mum and partner, with whom she lived, to get home from work before going home herself. Vicki was at a loss to explain her anxiety and why being alone was so difficult. After some initial investigation, she recalled a troubled childhood. Her father left her and her mother one day without warning, never to be seen or heard from again. Her mum, saddled with huge debts run up by her father, was forced to work two jobs, and through necessity, Vicki was left alone in her house a lot of the time. Connecting her past and present enabled Vicki to make sense of her anxiety and move on with her life.

Looking back at your Meaning Map activities and their outcomes, I hope you can make better sense of why things are as they are by:

- building an effective relationship with your Emotional Self
- identifying your causes and how to respond
- aligning your past, present and future
- building a coherent narrative.

If you can't, remember you can always find someone new to talk to.

Observing Self

During my therapy training, I read a book by American psychiatrist, Arthur Deikman, called The Observing Self. The book explores what modern psychological practice can learn from how ancient, mystical traditions approached psychological healing. *The Observing Self* is a concept from Eastern traditions and the basis of Deikman's book.

Who or what is the 'Observing Self'? Well, we all have one, and my understanding is that the Observing Self is the same as our authentic or 'core' self. In other words, it is you and me, the chief, the boss, the decision maker. Our Observing Self is the part of us that oversees our lives and everything in them, who steps back, reflects on and sets things in motion. To repeat, your Observing Self is you. And who are you? You are someone who wants to thrive and survive by putting your problems behind you and succeeding at your transformation.

When we struggle in life and become trapped in negative patterns of thought, behaviour, feeling and relating, we can make sense of this by understanding that our Observing Self is no longer 'in charge'. Over the following pages, I will show you who does take over and why they are responsible for why things are as they are.

On page 46 is an illustration of how I use The Observing Self concept. Looking at it from your point of view, in the middle is your Observing Self and around them are what I call your 'sub-selves', who play specific roles in your life. As you will see, this distinction is crucial. Sub-selves are a part of who you are, but they are not who you are. The task of your Observing Self is to create harmony between your sub-selves and ensure they are fully supportive of you.

What should happen is this. As the boss, your Observing Self brings on individual sub-selves to play specific roles, ones their personality and characteristics make them suitable for. In doing so, your Observing Self swaps places with the chosen sub-self, temporarily relinquishing control of your life to them. When they have fulfilled their role, positions are reversed, and your Observing Self takes charge once more. So far, so good, but it doesn't always work out this way.

Introducing your Negative Self

Let me give you a scenario. One day during a difficult time in your life, one of your sub-selves, who I call your Negative Self (sub-self A in my illustration), was brought in by your Observing Self to play an appropriate role. However, when the time came for them to swap places and return to the periphery of your life, they refused because they enjoyed being in charge too much. Try as your Observing Self did that day, they lost out, and it was they who ended up on the periphery of your life. From that day onwards, your Negative Self took control of how you think, behave, feel and relate to the outside world and the people in it.

On page 24 in 'Looking in the wrong place', I listed the symptoms and effects below that we can experience when life becomes challenging and complex.

- Physical symptoms such as chest pain, stomach issues and headaches.
- Negative, intrusive thoughts.
- Difficult emotional states such as stress, anxiety, depression and anger.
- Problematic behaviours such as avoidance, procrastination or perfectionism.
- Unhealthy lifestyles such as alcohol dependency, drug use and overeating.
- Relationship problems such as irritability, conflict.
- Professional issues such as work-related stress.

No one chooses to inflict such misery on themselves, yet for many people, this is a reality made worse by an inability to make sense of it. This is where my version of the Observing Self concept comes in. It hands responsibility for these miserable symptoms and effects to our Negative Selves. Once they were given control, they piled on the negativity until our Observing Selves gave up any hope of resuming their position at the centre of our lives.

You are not your Negative Self

The greatest trick Negative Selves perform is to convince us that we are them, and they are us. As a practitioner, therefore, it is vital I demonstrate to clients that they are not their Negative Selves. Only then can they take back ownership of their identity, thoughts, behaviours, feelings and relationships. So how do I demonstrate to someone that they are not their Negative Self? I simply refer to their presence in my practice room. The thing about Negative Selves is they never act against their own interests. Ever heard of the phrase, 'Turkeys don't vote for Christmas'? Well, Negative Selves don't book coaching or therapy sessions or facilitate anything that could lead to them being sent back where they came from—the periphery of our lives. People like me and books like this represent a threat to the dominance of Negative Selves. They didn't buy this book; you did. They aren't still reading; you are. And they aren't the ones intent on thriving and surviving... you get the idea.

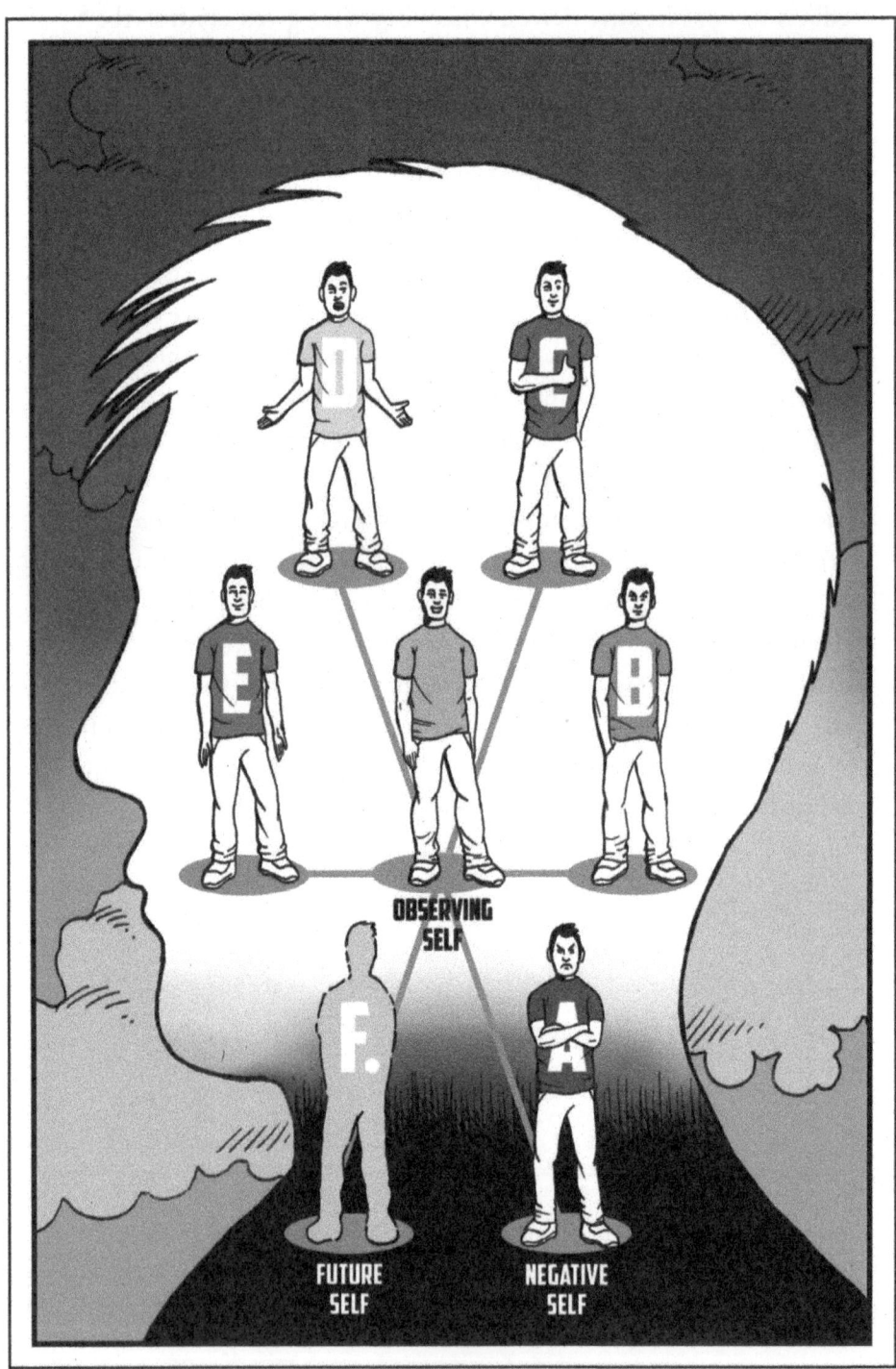

THE OBSERVING SELF

The Observing Self activity

My Observing Self activity will help you make further sense of why things are as they are by showing you how your Negative Self has been hindering your ability to thrive and survive.

In the illustration is your Observing Self and surrounding by sub-selves, including your Negative Self (Self A). Between them are the 'mental' bridges that allow each of them to swap places and which your Negative Self refused to go back across on that fateful day. I have featured six sub-selves, but you can have as many or as few as you like. Notice they all have different facial expressions to help you decide which part of you they represent. If you want to regain control of your life, ideally, you want a group of sub-selves who possess the attributes that will make this possible. When I do this activity with clients, they are often surprised they have a group of sub-selves so clever have their Negative Selves been in hiding them from view.

Now that you have been introduced, or more accurately reintroduced, to your sub-selves, the next step is to bring them to life by giving each of them their own name, personality, characteristics and role. Note you are doing this for your Negative Self too, but this time you will be telling them who they are, not the other way around. The list of sub-selves below is an example from one of my clients, but bring yours to life in ways that truly reflect who you want them to be.

- A. Negative Self.
- B. Optimistic Self.
- C. Compassionate Self.
- D. Helpful Self.
- E. Determined Self.
- F. Future Self.
- G. Resilient Self.

You are welcome to rename your Negative Self as well. One young lady I worked with successfully overcame her shopping addiction by labelling her Negative Self as 'The Crazy Bitch'. While I am not suggesting you use such colourful language, personalising your Negative Self can prove highly effective because it can create greater separation between them and you.

A note on 'F'. 'F' is your Future Self and is dotted deliberately because you are always becoming them without actually being them. 'F' is, perhaps, the most critical sub-self because as you get older, they take on the personalities and roles of the others, including your Observing Self. This is why you must separate from your Negative Self because if you don't, they will ensure that 'F' becomes more negative the older you get. With your Observing Self in charge surrounded by a cast of positive sub-selves, 'F' can become who you want them to be.

Taking each sub-self, complete the following activity, paying attention to the tenses used. Notice I use the past tense for your Negative Self i.e., 'got'; the present tense for your other sub-selves; and the future tense for sub-self, 'F', i.e., 'will'. Using tenses in this way marks the beginning and end of your Negative Self's reign by consigning them to your past.

- My Negative Self (enter a new name, if they have one), got me to:
    - think like this
    - behave like this
    - feel like this
    - relate like this.

- My sub-self B is called (enter name), and they:
    - think like this
    - behave like this
    - feel like this
    - relate like this.

- My sub-self C, D, E etc., are called (enter names), and they:
    - think like this
    - behave like this
    - feel like this
    - relate like this.

- My Future Self, F (you can rename them too if you want), will:
    - think like this
    - behave like this
    - feel like this
    - relate like this.

- My Observing Self is me, and I now:
    - think like this
    - behave like this
    - feel like this
    - relate like this.

What did you discover?

> "Even though I was in a senior leadership position in charge of one hundred or so people, the 'tag' of imposter was never far away. No matter how well I progressed professionally, I could hear that voice in my head telling me I was a fraud and didn't deserve to be here. For all of my life I believed that voice, and then, there it was beautifully expressed: tricked into believing I was an imposter by my negative self. I have done loads of leadership training, but this exercise nailed it for me."
> Karen

I hope that my Observing Self activity has put you back in charge and brought a group of sub-selves into your life that will play a crucial role in helping you achieve your transformation.

A note of caution. Negative Selves rarely appreciate being sent back to the edge of our lives, so expect them to protest in the strongest terms and make things difficult for you. Anticipate they will try to regain what they have lost by throwing everything they have at their disposal at you. Remember, they succeeded once and will feel confident about doing so again. The difference this time around, however, is you will be ready for them. From now on, whenever you think, behave, feel and relate in ways that undermine your thriving and surviving, you will know this is your Negative Self trying to lure you into their trap. Using what you have covered in this chapter, you can outwit them by being more intelligent and determined.

The Valuables Test

To wrap this chapter up, I will take you through my Valuables Test, which is a great way to defeat Negative Selves.

When on that fateful day, we let our Negative Selves hoodwink us into believing we were them, and they were us, we gave away our most valuable possession: our health and wellbeing. And yet if, at that time in our lives, a total stranger had asked us to hand over everything valuable we possessed, we would have said, "No!" Our house, car, money, technology or things of emotional value—none of it would we have given away. So why would we have fought to keep hold of our wallets, laptop and family photos but not our health and wellbeing? Because we didn't value ourselves enough. Only this explanation accounts for why we gave away the very thing upon which everything else depends, our health and wellbeing.

So we need to be ready. When our banished Negative Selves come along, which they will, and ask us to hand over everything of value we possess, as they did before, this time we will say, "No!" How we do so could go something like this:

Start by listing everything of value you possess. Once you have your list, spend some time connecting with your possessions. Remind yourself of what they mean to you. Now imagine a stranger or even someone you know but really don't like asking you to hand your possessions over to them. How do you feel? I hope you feel like saying, "No." Now locate in your mind and body where that 'No' resides. This is your 'place of certainty'. When your Negative Self comes along and asks you to hand over everything of value again, find your place of certainty, and stare them in the face. They want nothing more than to take away what you value. This time you won't let them.

Like stars and planets, placing value at the core of our system exerts a 'gravitational' effect on our thoughts, behaviours, feelings and relationships (to people, places and 'stuff'), pulling them into its orbit and harmony with it. Watching it happen is a thing of beauty.

Summary of chapter two

- o To overcome our difficulties, we need to make sense of why things are as they are.
- o An inability to find meaning shifts our focus to symptoms and effects, which are diagnostically unreliable.
- o The best source of meaning is our emotions, which are messages sent by our Emotional Selves.
- o Emotional Selves only communicate about one thing: our thriving and surviving, and how near or far we are from achieving this optimal state.
- o To make sense of our experiences, we need to align our past, present and future and construct a coherent narrative for our lives.
- o The Observing Self concept can enable us to make sense of negative ways of thinking, behaving, feeling and relating and put us back in control.
- o The Valuables Test can ensure we keep hold of what we value the most and do not give it away again.

P is for PATTERNS

Imagine the following two scenarios

Scenario one

I am looking at your difficulties under a microscope. What do I see? Initially, I see the outline of multiple patterns. Then as my eyes adjust and take in more of the finer detail, I see what the patterns consist of: separate but interwoven patterns of thought, behaviour, feeling and relating. Lifting my head from over the microscope, I engage you in conversation.

"What am I seeing?" I ask you.

"Oh, that's just who I am. It's what I do," you reply. "I'd rather be a different version of myself and do things differently, but somehow it never works out that way."

"But what if it did work out?" I persist, "what *might* I see?"

"Well," you say, "you'd see a different set of patterns."

Scenario two

I am looking at your difficulties under a microscope. What do I see? Initially, I see the rough outline of multiple patterns. Then as my eyes take in the finer detail, I see what the patterns consist of: separate but interwoven patterns of thought, behaviour, feeling and relating. Lifting my head from over the microscope, I engage you in conversation.

"What am I seeing?" I ask you.

"Oh, that's just who I am. It's what I do. I'm always looking to tweak and improve, fine-tune and strengthen."

"Great," I reply. "If I came back in six months? What might I see then?"

"Well," you say, "you'd see a new and improved set of patterns."

In this chapter, I aim to help you to:

- develop your understanding of what patterns are and the types that exist
- identify the unhelpful patterns in your life and how to replace them with helpful ones
- identify the helpful patterns in your life that you wish to develop further.

To get you started, I will ask you to read The Cliff Edge, a story of mine that resonates with people more often than not. Perhaps it is the visual nature of the story that engages the imagination. All I know is that it frequently increases self-awareness and produces valuable insight. Therefore, you might want to create some privacy by finding a quiet space without interruptions. Take a pen and paper to note what the story triggers for you.

P IS FOR PATTERNS

The Cliff Edge

You find yourself in an unfamiliar place. Although you try to get your bearings, the dense fog surrounding you makes this impossible. So thick is the fog, in fact, that when you put your hand up to your face, you can't see it. You stumble along when all of a sudden, the ground disappears from beneath your feet, and you fall into nothingness. Seconds pass, and still, you are dropping—you assume from a great height. *Thump!* You hit the ground. Coming to, you are bumped and bruised, but it appears no real damage is done.

Lying flat on the ground, you look up and reflect on what just happened. You decide not to give yourself a hard time because you had never been to that place before, and the fog made it doubly difficult, one of those unfortunate incidents.

The following day, you are back in the same place, although you don't know this yet. Today it is clear and sunny, and you can see for miles in every direction. Although this place looks unfamiliar—you don't recognise any part of the landscape—you have a gut feeling that you have been here before. Walking for a short while, you notice something up ahead. As you get closer, what you see is a cliff edge! The penny drops, and your gut instinct makes sense. "Ah!" you exclaim. This is where you were yesterday when the ground disappeared beneath your feet.

A few seconds later, you hit the ground with a thump. It takes you a while to figure out what happened, but only one conclusion presents itself: you went over the cliff edge again. This time your reflections are altogether different. While yesterday you can understand why you went over, it does not make sense at all today. After all, you saw the cliff edge before you got to it and yet, for reasons best known to yourself, over you went. The bumps and bruises are more severe this time, and yesterday's forgiving tone has been replaced by something far more critical. In fact, you give yourself a hard time.

Next day and you are back. There is something very seductive about this place, something that is drawing you back. You know

THE CLIFF EDGE

exactly where you are, of course. Up ahead is the cliff edge. Suddenly your brain registers that your right foot is no longer in contact with the ground. Adrenaline rushes through your body, and you throw yourself backwards, landing with much less of a thump a metre or so away from the cliff edge. "Phew! That was close," you say.

The awareness of what you have just prevented begins to register with you. "If I am to return to this place, and I accept that I must, I can't keep going over that cliff edge." You give it another glance and shake your head. Getting to your feet, your gaze takes in the panorama of the landscape—a beautiful landscape. A question comes to mind. If I am not going over the cliff, then where am I going? Your gaze sweeps the landscape again and settles on a spot not too far away. An intense feeling, more intense than the one that kept bringing you back to the cliff edge, connects itself to the spot not too far away. It is a feeling of hope and potential.

"I'm going over there," you say to yourself. Mentally, you trace a path from where you are now to where you want to be. A few seconds later, you are on that path. The cliff edge still exerts its influence, and you feel its pull at times, but like a fraying rope at breaking point, it becomes a weak tether. The further down the path you travel, the stronger the pull of 'over there' becomes. And then it dawns on you in a moment of true liberation that you will never go over that cliff edge again.

What is a Cliff Edge?

A Cliff Edge is anything we do a lot of that isn't working.

What is an 'Over There' place?

An 'Over There' place is where we do a lot of what is working. It is the place we go to when we are no longer going over our cliff edges, where we are who we want to be, doing what we want to be doing and living the life we want to be living.

What is a pattern?

In my IMPACT Model, patterns are anything that regularly feature in our lives that either enhances our thriving and surviving or undermines it. Patterns can be 'internal' to us, such as patterns of thought, or external to us, such as patterns of relationships (to people, places and 'stuff'). They can, of course, be both e.g., when we think of one person while engaging with another.

How do patterns form?

Patterns in our lives are a combination of innate (what we are born with – nature) and learnt (what we acquire from others and learn by ourselves – nurture) patterns. Take language. Nature gives us a head start, and then we build on it through nurture. Sometimes this process works to our advantage, and sometimes the opposite is true. This chapter focuses on understanding how to encourage the former and avoid the latter.

Unhelpful patterns form for positive reasons

It will not surprise you that helpful patterns form for positive reasons, but what might do is that unhelpful patterns form for positive reasons too. So, I want this to be your working assumption: unhelpful patterns that have become established in your life will have done so for beneficial reasons i.e., they will have made enough of a difference at the time. A common example is overeating to cope with stress or unhappiness. In this chapter, we will look at resolving this contradiction, but for now, I will leave you with this thought. While one part of you might know if a pattern is harmful, others might not know or even care. Which other parts of you, I hear you ask? Well, you have already been introduced to them: your Observing Self and your sub-selves. Your Observing Self and positive sub-selves might not know about your unhelpful patterns because your Negative Self has deceived them. And your Negative Self won't care because a life driven by unhelpful patterns suits them just fine.

Awareness is key

Awareness is key to identifying, understanding and changing patterns. If we are unaware, we might think there isn't anything to correct or improve, or we might mistake partial for complete awareness and fail to see enough of a pattern. As we covered in chapter two, the less we know about matters of importance, the more our Emotional Selves will make themselves heard. If we are experiencing difficult emotions such as stress, anxiety and depression, there is a good chance our Emotional Selves are unimpressed by our levels of awareness. Like a light being turned on in the darkness, awareness allows us to have a good look at our patterns and ask essential questions, such as:

- what am I doing a lot of that isn't working and that I will need to stop or do much less of?
- What am I not doing enough of that is working and that I will need to build and develop?

I hope that by the end of this chapter, you will be able to answer these questions in ways that enhance your ability to thrive and survive.

Types of patterns

Below are the main types of patterns I come across in my work. Consider the list and take some time to answer my questions, adding any of your own as you do so. (At this stage, don't get into assessing your patterns as being good or bad, right or wrong, positive or negative. You will get to do this later in my Cliff Edge activity.) Remember to keep my definition of a pattern in mind: anything that regularly features in our lives that either enhances our thriving and surviving or undermines it.

- Attention: where do you focus your attention? Who or what

gets the lion's share?
- Thinking: what do you think about? How would you describe your thinking style?
- Believing: what beliefs do you hold about yourself and the world around you?
- Behaving: what actions and behaviours do you carry out? What are your routines?
- Feeling: what emotions do you experience? Which are typical for you?
- Relating: what types of relationships do you form with people, places and 'stuff' i.e., objects, possessions?
- Time: how do you manage your time? Can you prioritise or not?
- Physical: what postures do you adopt? How do you move and express yourself physically?
- Transformation: how do you approach your academic, personal and professional transformation?

Doing, causing or occurring patterns

Another way I think about patterns is in terms of 'doing, causing and occurring'. Doing and causing patterns I see as:

- anything someone does or causes that is either helpful or unhelpful.

Occurring patterns I see as:

- anything occurring to someone that is either helpful or unhelpful.

By labelling patterns in these two ways, I am distinguishing between those someone knows they do or cause in some way—even if they don't understand why—and those that happen or appear to happen to someone inexplicably or without them realising. These types reflect my professional experience working with patterns and

can be broken down further into those someone:
- knows they do or cause and knows why
- knows they do or cause without knowing why
- knows they occur without realising the role they play in them
- is entirely unaware of.

"When my wife suggested I was eating too much, I took offence. So she got my jeans and suit trousers from the wardrobe and told me to put them on. I couldn't. I remember bursting into tears. Then the real showstopper. My wife showed me a diary she had been keeping of my eating habits. When I saw Mark, and we did some work on my patterns, I was able to see my journey from total unawareness to fully knowing that I did and caused them, and importantly why—because I was unhappy."
David

As David discovered, developing a good understanding of our pattern types is critical. If we know we do or cause our unhelpful patterns and why it is much easier to interrupt (more on this shortly) and replace them with helpful ones. Conversely, if we know we do or cause our helpful patterns and why it is simpler to reinforce them or lay down new ones.

As a coach and therapist, I know people often don't take credit for the positive patterns in their lives or believe they can do anything about the negative ones. This is a shame because they should and can.

Past, present and future patterns

A third way I think about pattern types is their connection to our past, present and future. Although our awareness and experience of patterns occur in the present, it can be helpful to know their past, present and future makeup when replacing or transforming them. In chapter two on Meaning, I suggested that 'misdiagnosis' of past, present and future when trying to make sense of why things are as they are, can lead us to 'look in the wrong place'. The same idea applies to working effectively on patterns. If I am working with a client's pattern of overeating, to be effective, I need to know if it is solely or primarily associated with, for example, past trauma, present job insecurity or future financial concerns. Similarly, for you, gaining such knowledge of what could be driving and underpinning your patterns would—will—be incredibly useful.

So how do we get to know? By asking great questions like those below. Questions such as these can help you think about your patterns from a past, present or future perspective. Refer to page 60 and 61 list of pattern types to prompt you.

- What past patterns do you want to bring with you, and what do you want to leave behind?
- What present patterns are not working well for you that need addressing?
- What present patterns are working well for you that need maintaining or improving?
- Are there any emerging present patterns that, if allowed to develop, might become problematic for you?
- Are there any emerging present patterns that you like the look of that you can nurture and encourage?
- What patterns would you like and not like to see if you travelled into your future?

A combination of good diagnosis and great questions can elicit valuable knowledge and information with which to build helpful patterns (more of this later).

How can I tell if my patterns are helpful or unhelpful?

If it isn't obvious to us already that our patterns are helpful or unhelpful, luckily, we have a fail-safe mechanism to fall back on: our emotions. Yes, our Emotional Selves are very interested in our patterns because they are critical to our thriving and surviving and take a dim view of any that undermine it. Consequently, unhelpful patterns are always accompanied by emotional messages such as stress, anxiety, depression or anger. The opposite will be true, of course, for helpful patterns. When it comes to your patterns, your Emotional Self needs you to understand the following:

- they exist in the first place
- what their type is
- whether they are helpful or unhelpful
- what you will do to ensure they support your thriving and surviving.

The Cliff Edge activity

My Cliff Edge activity will help you put together what we have covered so far. To recap the story, it captures the moment of awareness when you stop going over your Cliff Edges and travel down the path to your Over There place, where you are who you want to be, doing what you want to be doing and living the life you want to be living. This activity fits in when you jump back from your Cliff Edge and save yourself from another bruising landing. It is when you become acutely aware that you cannot afford to keep repeating your unhelpful patterns or neglect your helpful ones.

To get the most out of the activity, here are some suggestions for how to go about it:

- do the activity more than once, with gaps in between, as it can take time to become helpfully aware of our patterns.
- consider the areas of your life impacted by your patterns

that you think are relevant by revisiting The Meaning Map activity from chapter two.
- do the activity yourself and, if possible, with trusted others who know you well.

Appreciate your findings regardless of what you discover. It doesn't matter at this stage how often you are going over your Cliff Edges, only that you become aware of doing so.

Patterns	Unhelpful patterns: going over your Cliff Edges	Helpful patterns: in your Over There place	Do, cause or occur?	Past, present or future? Combinations of?
Attention: where, who and on what?				
Thoughts: what you think about and your thinking style				
Beliefs: about yourself and the world				
Behaviours: actions and routines				
Emotions and feelings				

Patterns	Unhelpful patterns: going over your Cliff Edges	Helpful patterns: in your Over There place	Do, cause or occur?	Past, present or future? Combinations of?
Relationships: to people, places and 'stuff' (objects, possessions)				
Time management and prioritisation				
Physical posture, movement and expression				
Academic, personal and professional transformation				

What did you discover?

Depending on your starting point i.e., how well or otherwise you understood your patterns, what did you gain from the activity? Were initial suspicions confirmed, or were you surprised by your discoveries? Are you going over more Cliff Edges than is good for you? Or is your Over There place closer than you realised? If you get stuck, use my client Sarah's completed version below to help:

Pattern types	Unhelpful patterns: going over your Cliff Edges	Helpful patterns: in your Over There place
Attention: where, who, and on what?	Excessive social media use; following several influencers; non-stop comparing to others	Professional attention is much better; never lose track at work
Thoughts: what you think about and your thinking style	I am failing at everything and others are succeeding; highly damaging, self-critical	Clarity of thought at work; can keep personal and professional separate
Beliefs: about yourself and the world	I will never achieve in life; I will never be happy	Can't think of any, but perhaps I am good at my job?
Behaviours: actions and routines	Doom scrolling on mobile phone; excessive exercising, constant dieting; self-sabotage	Very productive and organised at work
Emotions and feelings	Low moods, anger	Fake happiness. Numbness
Relationships: to people, places and 'stuff' (objects, possessions)	People-pleasing; hang around in places, especially gyms, to boost self-esteem	Cooperative, collaborative and supportive at work; I like being at work
Time management and prioritisation	Personally, non-existent	Professionally, on it
Physical posture, movement and expression	Tense, stiff; people ask me if I am ok because I look angry	I can be relaxed when absorbed in a task

Pattern types	Unhelpful patterns: going over your Cliff Edges	Helpful patterns: in your Over There place
academic, personal and professional transformation	Never happy with what I have achieved. Always looking to the next course, job, promotion to make me happy, but it never does	Objectively, I know I have achieved and that seeking new developmental opportunities is a good thing

Laying down helpful patterns

The rest of the chapter will focus on how you can interrupt and fatally weaken unhelpful patterns and lay down strong, helpful ones that will keep your Emotional Self happy and contented.

The Potter's Wheel and The Hammer

When you bring to mind a pattern and what it consists of, it is critical that you see it as something that can be worked on and that you have the tools with which to do so. Here are two analogies to help illustrate this idea.

- If you think of a pattern like a painting on the wall, it remains unchanged no matter how often you stare at it. But if you see it as a piece of clay on a potter's wheel, it becomes something to shape and reshape into something you like the look of.
- If you have a hammer, you can do one of two things with it: bash yourself over the head or build something great. The ability to build patterns is a tool like a hammer (clue: it's not the hammer that decides how and for what it is used).

If unhelpful patterns are dominating your life, it follows that you are:

- spending too much time in your 'mental' art gallery

- being splattered with clay spinning from your potter's wheel
- depending on painkillers to get rid of self-inflicted head injuries.

You have the ability and tools to lay down helpful patterns to support your thriving and surviving. Appreciating the significance of this idea cannot be underestimated.

Pattern matching

Pattern matching is a process whereby information coming in through our senses in the present is 'pattern matched' to information and knowledge we have already got 'stored' in our mind/body systems. Pattern matching involves what we experience externally through sight, sound, touch, taste and smell and internally through thoughts, feelings and physical sensations. Practical understanding and use of pattern matching can ensure we shape and reshape our clay into something we like the look of and build something solid and sturdy with our hammer.

Given the subject of this book, the focus here is on emotionally significant information i.e., that which our mind/body systems recognise as being relevant to us for our thriving and surviving, for either positive or not-so-positive reasons. When your mind/body system takes in new, emotionally significant information, I want you to imagine it is asking itself a series of questions, such as:

- what is this information, and what does it mean to my owner? For example, is it positive or negative?
- What is this information, and what does it mean for my owner? For example, are their lives about to change for the better or for the worse?
- What does my owner usually do with this information? How do they typically respond? For example, are they active or passive?
- This new information looks like that past information.

Should I use the past as a precedent? Or should I reclassify the information and break the link between past and present?

Once it has asked these questions, your mind/body system turns to you for guidance. What do you want me to do with this information? What does it mean to you? How will you respond? At this point, pattern matching becomes a critical process to understand and use because how we engage with our mind/body systems and answer their questions determines what happens to our patterns. To illustrate, consider the following case study and scenarios.

- **We don't know our mind/body system is asking us questions, meaning we fail to respond. Consequently, our silence is taken as confirmation by our mind/body system that it can use our past as a precedent. The outcome? Existing patterns are reinforced.** Chris is struggling at work. Every time he goes to call a client, he has a panic attack. Simply looking at his phone is enough to trigger intense panic. Chris is entirely unaware that his mind/body system is pattern-matching each new client call to a disastrous one he made a year ago when he lost a major deal to a competitor. When Chris fails to respond to its questions, his mind/body system uses the past as precedent and runs the 'disaster' pattern, triggering a panic attack.
- **We do know our mind/body system is asking us questions, but our response confirms nothing has changed. The outcome? Existing patterns are reinforced.** Chris knows that his mind/body system is pattern matching each new call to the disaster one from a year ago, but because his confidence is shot to pieces, he informs his mind/body system that nothing has changed. As a result, the disaster pattern is run, triggering a panic attack.
- **We do know our mind/body system is asking us questions, and our response confirms that things have changed. The outcome? Old patterns are weakened, and

new ones are laid down. It has been a year since Chris' disaster call. Walking into his office, he warmly greets his colleagues. Sitting at his desk, Chris looks at his phone, rehearses what he wants to say to a client and calls them. Chris feels calm and confident, and the call goes well. When his mind/body system asked its questions: *What should I do with this information (the call he's about to make)? What does it mean to you? How will you respond?* Chris confirmed that he had moved on from his disaster call and that his past was no longer a useful guide. Instead, Chris directed his mind/body system to the sales training and executive coaching he had undergone and the many successful deals signed in recent months. Consequently, his mind/body system ran a calm and confident pattern.

Building a detailed picture: The Pattern Builder

Changing and educating how our mind/body systems pattern match so we can lay down new and improved patterns is made easier if we have a detailed picture of all of our patterns. Below is my Pattern Builder activity – a series of nine questions – that can help you to gather quality information about the unhelpful patterns you need to replace or upgrade and the helpful ones you need to lay down or strengthen. The first set of questions addresses unhelpful patterns, and the second set helpful ones. I have included how Chris might have answered these questions as he sought to explain, understand and overcome his panic attacks.

Unhelpful patterns

1. When, where and with who were you when your unhelpful patterns started?
   Chris: "My panic attacks began immediately after my disaster call. I was in my office alone, talking to a particular client."

2. What stressors or changes were occurring in your life around the start of your unhelpful patterns?

    Chris: "Looking back, I realise I had been neglecting the client in question. If I am being honest, I had been avoiding them because they intimidated me. This is why the negotiation was a car crash."

3. How often do your unhelpful patterns occur, and how long do they last?

    Chris: "It's hard to say, but I think a panic attack usually lasts about ten or fifteen minutes. But the effects never really go away as I feel anxious and on the verge of panic all of the time."

4. What significant person(s) are present or absent when your unhelpful patterns occur?

    Chris: "It mainly happens when I think about or talk to clients at work, but sometimes when I am alone or with friends or family and the conversation is about work."

5. Where do your unhelpful patterns occur?

    Chris: "At work, especially in my office, but also at home on a Sunday evening before work, and in the car whenever I am travelling to and for work."

6. What are the steps involved in the generation of your unhelpful patterns? Put another way, can you identify the stages where you go from not doing your unhelpful patterns to doing them?

    Chris: "That's easy. Whenever I think about a client, I know I have to call or meet. Just looking at my diary or getting a reminder on my phone can trigger a panic attack. If I can, I take myself off to sit in a toilet cubicle and try to calm down. Then I force myself back into the office and make the call or get in the car. By then, I can be a wreck. Clients often ask me if I am ok, and I have to make up a reason for why I am acting oddly."

7. When do your unhelpful patterns not occur?
   Chris: "That's a hard question. Sometimes I talk to my manager or colleague before a client call. They think I am doing a bit of strategising, but in reality, I am just trying to stop myself from panicking. However, a call can go better when I do. Mmm, that's interesting. It hadn't occurred to me that some calls went better than others."
8. What do you think other people know about your unhelpful patterns e.g., managers and colleagues, family and friends?
   Chris: "I honestly don't know. I haven't been able to talk to anyone about my issues. I think they would be supportive. Again, that's interesting. Why would I not ask for support?"
9. What are your beliefs about your unhelpful patterns? For example, 'I can never change them' or 'I am to blame'?
   Chris: "I am a failure and a coward for letting this client intimidate me. I am not helping myself, am I?"

In answering these questions, Chris now has lots of useful information and knowledge to lay down new, helpful patterns. For example, he knows:

- why he is having panic attacks
- all of his client relationships started to deteriorate after an original 'disaster' call with one in particular
- the problematic client relationship was based on patterns of fear and intimidation, resulting in those of avoidance and concealment (from supportive others)
- he has more effective client calls when he gets support beforehand
- he needs to seek support from others to regain his confidence and self-belief.

Over to you. Use examples from your Cliff Edge activity and ask yourself the same nine questions to build a detailed picture of your unhelpful patterns.

Helpful patterns:

Regardless of what you discovered above, it is vital that you answer both sets of questions. Even if you believe you don't have any helpful patterns, you must establish whether this is true. If it isn't true and you do have some helpful patterns, you are in a better position than you realised. However, if you prove your belief, answering the questions can enable you to build up a picture of what your patterns would look like if they were helpful. To help, refer back to times when you were in a good place. What were your patterns like then? Just because this period might not be your best doesn't mean you don't have a library of helpful patterns to take inspiration from. Or, if you can't recall any positive periods, formulate answers opposite to those from your first set of questions.

1. When, where and with who were you when your helpful patterns started?
   Chris: "My helpful patterns started when I finally accepted that I was in trouble and needed support. I remember having another panic attack in my car before work and deciding enough was enough."
2. What factors or changes were occurring in your life around the start of your helpful patterns?
   Chris: "I started to let people in rather than push them away. In other words, I was changing. I wanted a better life for myself and my family."
3. How often do your helpful patterns occur, and how long do they last?
   Chris: "Now, they last virtually all the time because I know how to sustain them. I still have off days but am much better at spotting and handling them now."
4. What significant person(s) are present or absent when your helpful patterns occur?
   Chris: "Well, I am always present, which feels great, but my coach and manager are always on hand should I need them.

I used to have one or two negative people in my life, but no longer."

5. Where do your helpful patterns occur?
   Chris: "Work, especially when I am with clients doing what I love doing the most: selling and winning business. My home life has benefited massively, too. I am more present and engaged with my partner and children."

6. What are the steps involved in the generation of your helpful patterns? Put another way, can you identify the stages where you go from not doing your helpful patterns to doing them?
   Chris: "As I said above, I definitely have off days. When I am struggling, I acknowledge this and use self-talk to remind myself that I have been here before and recovered. If this isn't enough, I speak to my manager or coach."

7. When do your helpful patterns not occur?
   Chris: "The only time is when I take on too much when I should be saying 'No' instead of 'Yes.'"

8. What do you think other people know about your helpful patterns e.g., managers and colleagues, family and friends?
   Chris: "Now, they know everything—because I tell them. The days of hiding myself away are over."

9. What are your beliefs about your helpful patterns? For example: 'I have worked hard to establish them' or 'I know how to sustain them.'
   Chris: "I am proud of myself for having turned my life around, and I no longer fear bad days or periods because I am much more resilient."

What did you discover? How has The Pattern Builder changed what you knew or didn't know about your patterns? What can you do with the detailed pictures you have built? Where does your focus need to be?

The strongest source of emotion

The key to laying down new, helpful patterns is to make them more emotionally persuasive than old, unhelpful ones. Unless and until this happens, nothing will change because our mind/body systems lock on to patterns with the strongest source of emotion. Remember, old, unhelpful ones, will have formed for 'positive' reasons i.e., they made enough of a difference to our lives at the time. Left unchallenged, the positivity of old patterns is reinforced by the twin forces of time and repetition. Ever wondered why most New Year's Resolutions fail? Now you have the explanation.

Unfortunately, our mind/body systems can be very uncritical of even the most unhelpful patterns. Their working assumption is that patterns retain their original positivity unless they hear otherwise from us. What persuades our mind/body systems to replace old, unhelpful patterns with new, helpful ones is evidence, lots of concrete evidence, that new patterns are more positive and beneficial. When we find the evidence, though, something beautiful happens: old, unhelpful patterns are replaced.

Building evidence: The Valuables Test revisited

So how do we build enough evidence to persuade our mind/body systems? The key is protecting what we value the most: our health and wellbeing. When we do this, the evidence builds automatically.

In chapter two (MEANING), on page 50, I introduced you to my Valuables Test, which emphasised the significance of value in achieving change. When old, unhelpful patterns trump new, helpful ones, we lose value, but reversing this process protects and grows it. And this is where the magic happens because refusing to give away what we value automatically results in decisions that produce the evidence our mind/body systems needs.

"The Valuables Test showed me why my New Year's Resolutions always failed. It wasn't for the lack of trying because I

tried every year to change my life. My decision to work with Mark to change careers and a personal trainer to get in shape happened when I stopped giving my value away. My old patterns of professional paralysis and weight gain, which had plagued me for years, fell away remarkably easily under the weight of new evidence."
Lisa

As Lisa discovered, understanding the connection between value, decision-making, and evidence-building makes it easier for us to:

- make value-based decisions that support our thriving and surviving
- gather the evidence we need to persuade our mind/body systems
- replace old, unhelpful patterns with new, helpful ones
- keep our helpful patterns in good shape.

If you are still unsure or unpersuaded about the benefits of your new, helpful patterns versus your old, unhelpful ones, then use the activity in the table below and subject them to comparison. Aim to build the case for new patterns by interrogating the supposed benefits of your old ones.

Positives and benefits of old patterns	Positives and benefits of new patterns
Pattern 1	Pattern 1
Pattern 2	Pattern 2

Positives and benefits of old patterns	Positives and benefits of new patterns
Pattern 3	Pattern3

Pattern Interruption

When my eldest daughter was a baby, she often made life difficult for her father by refusing to drink her milk. On one particular occasion, when she had declined the offer of milk for the umpteenth time, I decided to mix things up. Instead of staying at home, I took her to a baby changing room at our local supermarket, where to my great relief, she drank her milk with no opposition. While she quickly got wise to my cunning, I saw how effective pattern interruption could be that day.

Pattern interruption is the addition of a new element or elements to an unhelpful pattern to change it into a helpful one. There are three main ways this can be done:

- by changing how we view unhelpful patterns
- by changing how we do or carry out unhelpful patterns
- by introducing and using resources.

These three principles can be broken down further into the following techniques and strategies. The accompanying examples are from clients I have worked with and how they have made pattern interruption work powerfully for them.

- Time
    - change how often unhelpful patterns are carried
    - do them more quickly or slowly

- o   vary when they happen
- o   change how long they take.

Phillip agreed to answer calls from his demanding mother every four days rather than straightaway, giving him back a sense of control of his life.

Lizzie agreed to 'speed' worry around her house, going from room to room as quickly as possible, stressing at 'top speed'. The result? She started laughing instead of worrying.

Freya's low self-esteem meant she felt exposed when holding her head high in public, so she started going out at less busy times with her head up, then proceeded to go out at increasingly busy times, increasing her self-confidence as she did so.

Jeff dedicated a particular time of day to grieve for his wife rather than engaging randomly with his thoughts about her whenever they came to mind.

- Space and place

  - o   change where unhelpful patterns occur
  - o   change how the space is arranged through movement and positioning of objects/contents
  - o   add new objects and contents into the space.

Adrian, a student, moved the scissors he self-harmed with from the bedroom of his shared house to the communal kitchen, which resulted in a significant reduction in his self-harm and its eventual end.

Beth tackled her self-esteem issues by applying make-up in a friend's room before a night out rather than her own, where she found it too difficult. Consequently, Beth socialised more often, boosting how she felt about herself.

Martin started to do more work from a local café because working from home negatively impacted his productivity.

Harriet addressed her belief she was unlikeable by sticking photos of friends to her fridge door to remind her that not only did she have friends, but that they liked her too.

- Order and sequence
    - vary the order of elements or stages of unhelpful patterns
    - break them down into smaller stages.

Teresa agreed to put on her favourite shoes when she needed to binge on food, which meant she found it much harder to go through with it.

Marc began his journey to giving up cocaine and ecstasy by handing his car keys to a friend. This meant that if he wanted drugs, he was faced with the prospect of a long trip by public transport. Much to his surprise, Marc discovered that drugs weren't that important.

Rita overcame her fear of motorway driving by starting on quieter roads and, with a trusted instructor, spending increasing amounts of time on busier roads until she lost her fear.

Geeta processed a traumatic event by interspersing it with hilarious clips from her favourite Charlie Chaplin movies. Every time she felt panicky, she played one of the videos to bring her emotional arousal down, thus 're-educating' her mind/body system so that it no longer needed to consider the relevancy of what she had been through.

- Positives and negatives
    - combine unhelpful patterns with unrewarding activities or outcomes
    - combine helpful patterns with rewarding activities or outcomes.

Jane overcame the obsessive checking of her university assignments by agreeing to hop up and down on one leg 100x if she checked her work more than three times. She also decided that if she limited her checks to three times and handed her work in, she could reward herself with a cup of green tea (Jane's idea of heaven).

Sarah agreed to make her four housemates breakfast in bed for a week if she failed to get up and go to university. The upshot? Jane had to make good on her promise when she stayed in bed the first morning but found that 'serving' her friends and the laughter it generated transformed her mood and motivation for her studies.

Rich agreed to lose or keep his Saturday night 'in front of the TV real ale and takeaway' (Rich's phrase) depending on whether he made the necessary commitment to controlling his anger.

- Change the context
    - change how unhelpful patterns are understood
    - change what they mean
    - change their conditions.

Sharon agreed to hand over her treasured mobile phone to a friend who was under strict instruction to give it back only after she had been to the gym. The outcome? Sharon's resistance to exercise was replaced by enjoyment of it.

Raj, who was in grave danger of failing his Master's Degree for no good reason other than 'laziness', told his parents (he actually called them during a coaching session) that if he didn't turn things around, they were not to pay for his snowboarding holiday. Raj graduated and went on his winter holiday.

Matt stopped driving himself to achieve unsustainable levels of performance at work after he realised that doing so was part of a broader people-pleasing pattern connected to his difficult upbringing.

- Change the makeup or blueprint
    - observe unhelpful patterns as they are being carried out
    - comment and reflect on them
    - add surprising or unexpected elements.

Just a single example here, but one that sticks in my memory. I once worked with a stepfather (his name escapes me) of two teenage daughters. When he came to see me, their relationship had entirely deteriorated, with mutual hatred on both sides. He said he was hated for not being their father, a reality he felt powerless to change. In therapy, I established that verbal requests, for example, "Can you do the washing-up, please?" were particular triggers of conflict. The solution he came up with was? He acquired a flipchart stand and paper from work, placed it in the kitchen, wrote out his 'polite requests' and left the room. What happened surprised them all. Removing the verbal element of the exchanges with his stepdaughters reduced the emotional temperature. Left to do chores alone, the two teenagers became more amenable to their stepfather's requests. Over time their relationship improved as each could see how hard the other was trying.

The Cliff Edge revisited

Having reached the end of the Patterns chapter and, hopefully, learnt more about the importance and impact of patterns in your life, complete the slightly amended Cliff Edge activity below. Ask yourself why and how you will be spending less time going over your Cliff Edges and more time in your Over There place.

Patterns	Cliff Edges	Over There
Attention: where, who and on what?	e.g., "I will avoid this Cliff Edge because…"	e.g., "I will go to my Over There place because…"
Thoughts: what you think about and your thinking style		
Beliefs: about yourself and the world		

Patterns	Cliff Edges	Over There
Behaviours: actions and routines		
Emotions and feelings		
Relationships: to people, places and 'stuff' (objects, possessions)		
Time management and prioritisation		
Physical posture, movement and expression		
Academic, personal and professional transformation		

A new relationship with unhelpful patterns

I wrote the two analogies below to help one client change their relationship with their unhelpful patterns, which have resonated with others ever since.

The wrong date

Imagine you are out one evening socialising with friends. Someone engages you in conversation and offers to buy you a drink. You politely decline their kind offer, making a mental note this person is *definitely* not your type. At the end of the evening, which included dinner with this person, you leave in a state of bafflement. "But they're not my type?" you say to yourself. The evening, you reflect, was depressing. A month and several dates later, you are amazed at how much time you spend with someone who offers you nothing.

And yet, here you are. Two holidays later, plans are being made to move in with this person. Nothing has changed. They are still not your type. In fact, they *really* irritate you. It's been a while since you last saw your friends. Five years pass, an engagement party and a date for your wedding... this would never happen to you, would it?

Two bouncers and a nightclub

Imagine your mind is a trendy nightclub. So trendy, in fact, that a long queue of clubbers forms and snakes down the road outside each night. They all want to get in and start dancing, but space on the dancefloor is at a premium. Your most trusted bouncers stand guard outside. The clubbers clamour, but not everyone gains entry. Cries of disappointment and tantrums leave your bouncers unmoved. At midnight, the bouncers turn their backs on the hordes and lock the doors—no more admissions. The dance floor is full, but there is room to groove. Everyone has a great time.

Summary of Chapter Three

- Patterns are anything that regularly features in our lives that is helpful or unhelpful.
- We can be aware or unaware of our patterns. Becoming aware of them is vital if we are to replace unhelpful patterns with helpful ones.
- The Cliff Edge story and activity can help you get to know your patterns.
- Pattern matching is how our mind/body systems compare new information coming in through our senses to old information stored 'up top' in our memory banks.
- Pattern interruption is how we 'interrupt' unhelpful patterns to lay down helpful ones.

A is for ACCEPTANCE

"Mark asked me why I walked so quickly, head down from the lift to my office. I said I didn't know I did and promptly burst into tears. Composing myself, I said with more honesty than I'd managed in a long time that I felt like an imposter, that I was a fake leader. The space between the lift and my office presented opportunities for my staff to 'out' me. My thinking was that I could use body language to communicate to everyone to leave me alone. Walking fast meant I could reach the sanctuary of my office and shut the door on the world. Mark listened to all this, paused, and asked a question that shook me to my core: 'When did I stop accepting myself?' I replied that I had never accepted myself."
Jessica

Many years ago, I saw a therapist to help me through a challenging period. In one particular session, my therapist sat back and observed: "You have to accept your reality. There is no choice in this." He said this because I was going around in circles after several sessions of therapy. I remember finding my therapist's comments irritating.

I was not interested in accepting my 'reality' because it was pretty bleak at the time. Why would I accept it?

I still see that therapist from time to time, not just because they are good at what they do, but also because they understood me better on that day than anyone else. They understood that I was afraid of accepting myself for who I was and my life for what it was. Rather than accept, I lived a fantasy existence until, with the support of someone who knew what I needed, I brought it to an end. This experience led me to develop my concept of helping people as I had been helped that day: The Fantasy-Reality Gap.

FANTASY / REALITY GAPS

Fantasy-Reality Gaps (FRGs)

Consider the following statements:

- who you are, and who you will be
- what you are doing, and what you will be doing
- how your life is, and how your life will be.

Understood in this way, FRGs are the difference between our current and future realities. We all have them because we all live in the present and all move towards the future. From this perspective, FRGs are normal and helpful as they map out the distance between our present and desired future, or 'fantasy', realities and the journeys to connect them.

My interest as a coach and therapist begins when FRGs become helpful or unhelpful, a division explained by the subjects of this chapter: acceptance and non-acceptance. As you shall see, acceptance results in 'helpful' FRGs that enable us to thrive and survive, and non-acceptance in 'unhelpful' FRGs, which undermine this ability.

As I discovered, it is the struggle or failure to accept our reality—who we are, what we do and the life we lead—that creates unhelpful FRGs. In this moment of disconnect, we automatically enter a 'fantasy' state and into conflict with ourselves and the world around us. The longer the conflict, the bigger the unhelpful FRGs become, and the more damage is done. This is why acceptance is so important. With it, we prevent unhelpful FRGs from opening up in the first place or shorten their duration and impact if they do. Without it, we deplete our mental and physical resources, fighting a losing battle between fantasy and reality.

My aim in this chapter is for my FRG concept to:

- explain difficulties and challenges in terms of acceptance and non-acceptance
- explain *your* difficulties in these terms
- help you find acceptance and overcome non-acceptance.

The FRG Spectrum: acceptance to non-acceptance

"I went to see Mark at a time when my eating habits were out of control. I had been a serial yo-yo dieter for years and had gone back and forth to various popular dieting clubs but always ended up putting any weight I had lost back on. I realised that there must be a reason why I felt the need to eat excessively, sometimes in secret, at times and longed to establish a normal relationship with food which I could sustain for life. Going back to a conversation we had in our first meeting Mark raised a point that sometimes people have a 'fantasy' about the person they are or want to be and I recall at the time that I did feel a little aggrieved by that comment but I actually think he hit the nail on the head. I have given this concept a lot of thought since then and have come to realise that there is a part of me who enjoys the idea of doing certain things more than the actual execution of it and actually, it is that part of me that sets the unrealistic and unachievable goals which then has a knock on effect with my poor eating habits and leads me to be unhappy and so the cycle continues. I am now learning to do what I actually enjoy doing, when I am able to do it and will focus on that for the time being. I am feeling very positive about the future and a lot more content with myself."
Emma

Before we look at FRGs and acceptance in greater detail, I will ask you to consider what you know and understand already. Whenever I do my FRG Spectrum activity with clients, they often surprise themselves with how much they do know.

Below, I have listed the three main types of FRG – who we are (identity), what we do (behaviour) and the life we lead (lifestyle) – and some accompanying statements. The first areas and statements are for helpful FRGs; the second are for unhelpful ones. Look down the list and then complete the activity.

Helpful FRGs:

- who I am, is who I think I am
- who I am, is who I want to be
- who I want to be, is who I can be
- what I am doing is what I think I am doing
- what I am doing is what I want to be doing
- what I want to do, is what I can do
- how my life is, is how I think my life is
- how my life is, is how I want my life to be
- how I want my life to be, is how my life can be

Unhelpful FRGs:

- who I am, is not who I think I am
- who I am, is not who I think I should be
- who I want to be, is not who I can be
- what I am doing is not what I think I am doing
- what I am doing is not what I think I should be doing
- what I want to do, is not what I can do
- how my life is, is not how I think my life is
- how my life is, is not how I think my life should be
- how I want my life to be, is not how my life can be.

As Emma articulated beautifully, FRGs become unhelpful when we struggle or fail to accept that things are not how we want them to be.

FRG activity

To get you thinking about FRGs and acceptance, consider which statements might apply to you. I say 'might' because you have only just been introduced to the FRG concept. For now, write down any statements you feel confident do apply to you, and make a 'best guess' for the others. In my experience, people create several lists before agreeing on a final one. When a friend of mine completed this activity, she said it took her two full days of reflection and made her 'reappraise my entire life.' While I am not suggesting you take two days, I am encouraging you to take your time because the subject of acceptance is so important.

What did you discover?

- Which FRG statements do you have more of, helpful or unhelpful ones?
- Is there a sub-category (identity, behaviour and lifestyle) you connected with the most? Or did you feel similar about all three?
- Where on the spectrum of acceptance (complete to none at all) does your statement list suggest you are?
- What does your list say about your relationship with acceptance?

Keep your list, thoughts and reflections so you can revisit them throughout the chapter.

How can I tell if I have helpful or unhelpful FRGs?

> "I spent years thinking I was someone who could form a certain type of relationship, a fantasy that years of disappointment and evidence to the contrary failed to dislodge. The FRG was a revelation not only because it opened my eyes to this fact but it also explained why I had been so angry and destructive for so long. How do I know this? Because my anger disappeared overnight when I accepted that who I was, was who I wanted to be."
> Francesca

Well, your list might be offering you some clues, but the determining factor is the current state of your life. In general terms, if we are thriving and surviving, there is a good chance our FRGs will be helpful or mainly helpful. Signs to look out for include personal and professional growth and positive mental health. In contrast, if we are struggling to thrive and survive and feel our life is 'in reverse', there is a good chance our FRGs will be unhelpful or mainly unhelpful. Signs to look out for include personal and professional stuckness and poor mental health.

However, we can be much more specific. Years of experience tell me that helpful and unhelpful FRGs have their own identifiable 'symptoms'. So, to remove any doubt about which of the two exists at the centre of your life, take a look at my FRG 'Symptoms Checker' on pages 93 and 94. In the lefthand column are the symptoms of unhelpful FRGs, and in the righthand column are those of helpful FRGs. Note down those you feel apply to you.

The FRG Symptom Checker

Signs of unhelpful FRGs	Signs of helpful FRGs
Poor mental health and wellbeing: Difficult emotions such as stress, anxiety, depression, anger, self-criticism, negative self-talk, negative thoughts, unwanted intrusive thoughts, negative, self-limiting beliefs low self-esteem, self-worth, low confidence negative memories, tiredness, fatigue, exhaustion, poor motivation, poor sleep.	**Good mental health and wellbeing:** Positive emotions such as joy, gratitude, interest, serenity, self-appreciation, positive self-talk, positive thoughts, a clear mind self-empowering beliefs, good level of self-esteem, self-worth, self-confidence, positive memories, high energy levels, quick recovery, resiliency, good levels of motivation, good sleep.
Negative behaviours: avoidance procrastination perfectionism fear of failure avoidance of risk-taking impatience frustration obsession compulsion addiction self-sabotage self-destruct denial secrecy poor self-care self-neglect.	**Positive behaviours:** engagement productive good enough stretched and challenged educated risk-taking setbacks are opportunities patience contentedness restraint control self-possession self-supporting openness honesty transparency good self-care.

Signs of unhelpful FRGs	Signs of helpful FRGs
Relationships (with self and others): critical, judgmental gameplaying blurred boundaries unconfident people-pleasing comparisons with others jealousy envy dismissive intolerant arrogant/self-promoting withdrawn avoidant argumentative irritable blaming issues with responsibility and accountability.	**Relationships (with self and others):** supportive, respectful relaxed clear boundaries assertive: I'm ok, you're ok acceptance and tolerance humility connection agreeable enjoyable approving responsible and accountable.
Unhelpful change strategies: unrealistic expectations quick fix rejection of support inflexibility – Plan A must work.	**Helpful change strategies:** realistic expectations commitment to doing what it takes seeking support flexibility – happy to switch to a Plan B.

What did you discover?

Can you see a relationship between your FRG statements and your 'symptoms'? Which of the following bests describes what you found?

- Acceptance is not an issue for me.
- Acceptance might be an issue for me.
- Acceptance is an issue for me.

Taking a closer look

If you think your FRGs are probably helpful, meaning you don't have particular difficulty with acceptance, it may be that the other stages of my IMPACT Model are more relevant for you. All I would say is that it will be worth staying with me to understand why your FRGs are helpful. However, if you believe your FRGs are probably unhelpful, indicating you do have issues with acceptance, then I am confident this next activity will prove informative, even enlightening.

The first FRG Spectrum activity asked about general FRGs. In this one, we will go into more detail. Below are the three main FRG areas of identity, behaviour and lifestyle broken down into more specific sub-categories (the list is not exhaustive, so if you think of one that I haven't, note this down too). As with your initial list of statements, note down those you feel might apply to you.

> "I liked to take drugs. It was my reward and my escape. There were downsides, but I pushed or tried to push those away. My fantasy was that I could be happy in myself, a good husband and father, a successful businessman and still smoke. The hard truth was that I couldn't and wasn't."
> Tony

Yourself:

- identity, gender, sexuality
- personal and professional role and status (do you 'matter'? Is what you do 'significant'?)
- beliefs (about yourself and the world around you)

- self-confidence, self-esteem and self-worth
- personal qualities and characteristics e.g.,
    - pessimism, optimism
    - honesty, generosity, likeability
    - introversion, extroversion
- physical appearance
- intellectual, emotional and social intelligence
- abilities, capabilities and skills
- strengths and weaknesses.

Your personal and professional circumstances:

- social e.g., level of social connectedness and participation
- cultural e.g., level of contribution to and participation in local and wider communities, such as volunteering, sport, religion and civic activity
- work and career
- personal and professional relationships
- financial and material
- past, present and future
- environment (where you live and work).

Your resources (internal and external):

- psychology:
    - optimism, pessimism
    - mindset
    - resilience
    - flexibility (thought, behaviour, feeling and relating)
    - insight, judgement
    - motivation

- o confidence, self-belief.

- mental and physical health, wellbeing
- money, wealth
- knowledge, experience and wisdom
- qualifications, competencies, training and skills
- people
- time
- information, knowledge, technology
- environment (access to what you need).

Your goals and objectives, dreams and aspirations

- personal/individual
- collective/joint
- academic
- professional.

Your strategies for achieving change, growth and transformation

- goal setting
- strategising, planning, preparation
- flexibility, adaptability
- realism, sustainability.

Awareness and discovery

"My fantasy boiled down to this. I didn't think I could leave my toxic partner, dead-end job or make any inroads into my chronically low self-esteem. Now I am back on the dating scene (aged 43) and thoroughly enjoying myself. I have a thriving video production business, and my self-esteem is consistently where I want it to be. Finding acceptance felt like receiving

an electric shock, but it marked the beginning of my transformation, just as Mark said it would."
Phillipa

- Which FRG sub-categories did you write down?
- Are there sub-categories you connected with the most?

Place this list alongside your first one (your general FRG categories) and answer the questions below.

- Where on the spectrum of acceptance do you think you are now?
- Have you moved from your original position or stayed put?
- Has your relationship with acceptance changed? For example, are you more or less accepting than you appreciated at the start of this chapter?

Now you have completed three acceptance activities (FRG Statements, FRG Symptom Checker, Taking a Closer Look), how is your thinking on the subject of acceptance developing? Are you:

- confirming what you already knew about your relationship with acceptance?
- Starting to acknowledge ideas about acceptance you have ignored or suppressed?
- In complete shock and surprise because you had no idea acceptance was an issue?

For some having a better understanding of acceptance and their FRGs can be positive, while for others, it can be daunting. Whatever your response, remember that finding acceptance is not a choice but a necessity because it is central to our:

- thriving and surviving
- mental health and wellbeing
- personal and professional transformation.

Prioritising your FRGs

If acceptance is an issue for you, the next step is to consider which specific FRG categories are the most unhelpful and which will need prioritising. Without a good understanding, we risk focusing on those that are less important or, worse, of no importance at all. Misdiagnosis of any problem can only make it worse.

So, taking your list of specific FRG sub-categories and using a 0–10 scale (0=very low priority, 10=very high priority), choose numbers that capture how you feel about each of them. As a general rule:

- scores of 7 or more indicate FRG categories requiring immediate attention
- scores of 5 or 6 indicate FRG categories requiring attention soon
- scores of 4 or below indicate FRG categories requiring a little nurturing or even leaving alone.

If necessary, repeat the activity more than once to identify your priority FRGs accurately.

Measuring your FRGs

To demonstrate your commitment to finding greater acceptance, you can also ask yourself what you would like to bring your numbers down to. What would this mean for you in terms of your:

- identity
- behaviour
- lifestyle.

For inspiration, look back at Phillipa's testimonial on page 97. She went from hating to liking herself, from being professionally unfulfilled to realising her entrepreneurial dreams, and from being in relationships that denied her individuality to ones that celebrated it.

Taking the priority areas you have identified, choose a number between 0 and 10 (0=in great shape, 10=in very poor shape) that represents where your unhelpful FRG is now, followed by a second number that represents where you would like it to be i.e., when it has become a helpful FRG.

- What is different about you?
- What are you doing differently?
- How is your life different?

The Black Hole Effect: living with unhelpful FRGs

As you have probably gathered by now, living with unhelpful FRGs is no fun at all. Like black holes, unhelpful FRGs pull the positivity from our lives and make it disappear, as it did with Damian, a university student I once worked with.

When we first met, Damian was far behind in his studies due to a combination of perceived 'laziness' and 'smoking far too much marijuana'. He was highly critical of himself and wanted my help to 'get a grip' because he was throwing his degree away. But this was a Fantasy.

Working through the Acceptance stage of The IMPACT Model enabled Damian to realise that none of his beliefs about himself were true. In therapy, he came to recognise that he was severely depressed and had been for most of his life due to sustained bullying at primary and secondary school. Once Damian accepted that his laziness, marijuana addiction, and lack of commitment were, in fact, unhelpful FRGs born out of trauma, he was able to make progress. (Damian graduated with a 2:1 in Journalism; when I last heard from him, he was in the early stages of a sports journalism career.)

'Why do FRGs become unhelpful?' The role of FRG types

None of us set out to undermine our lives by opening up unhelpful FRGs; it's just that this can happen for very 'human' reasons. Maybe we never knew about FRGs, or if we did, we lost sight of them in the busyness of our lives. Maybe adversity struck as it did for Damian. Or perhaps the significance of our dreams and ambitions and fear of failure overrode any warning signs. Whatever the reason, we can come to accept our 'fantasy' identities, behaviours and lifestyles as real and unwittingly create the conditions for further deterioration in our lives.

Types of unhelpful FRG

So far in this chapter, we have considered the importance of acceptance and how to identify, categorise and prioritise FRGs. In this section, I dig deeper into why unhelpful FRGs form by looking at individual types. Identifying types raises awareness, which is critical for replacing unhelpful FRGs with their helpful counterparts because it creates the conditions for acceptance. I will look at the issue of awareness in more detail later in the chapter, but for now, I will ask you to keep this observation in mind: when it comes to unhelpful FRGs, high levels of self-awareness are often noticeable for their absence.

Confidence

There are two types of Confidence FRGs: those created by a lack of confidence and those by an excess of it. Someone with an unconfident FRG will consistently underestimate themselves and what they are capable of. They will downplay who they are and what they do and prioritise the wants and needs of others (people-pleasing is a characteristic). Disappointment and failure are accepted as the norm, and any positives will be attributed to external factors such as luck or the sympathy of others and not to the efforts of the person themselves. Those with unconfident FRGs will also have a paradoxical relationship with success and achievement. They will strive hard to attain them (perfectionism is common), but accepting praise will feel difficult and uncomfortable. No limelight, please. Living with this type of FRG condemns someone to a life of unrealised potential.

- The Fantasy: someone believes they have no esteem and worth and lack the strengths and resources necessary to achieve in life and realise their potential
- The Reality: they do have esteem and worth, and they do possess the strengths and resources to succeed and demonstrate potential.

Conversely, someone with an over-confident FRG will overestimate themselves and what they are capable of. They will overplay their impact on others and the world around them, take success and achievement for granted and put any failure down to the inadequacies of those around them (who will often receive unfair and unjustified criticism). Personal or professional setbacks and lack of progress will result from unfairness and bias. And yet, like those with unconfident FRGs, someone with an overconfident FRG will also live a life of unrealised potential.

- The Fantasy: someone believes their esteem and worth are greater than they are and hold similar views regarding their strengths and resources, achievements and potential
- The Reality: they don't have the perceived levels of esteem and worth, or depth of strengths and resources, meaning that their expectations of success and measurement of potential are similarly exaggerated.

Stages of life

Tom was a newly qualified doctor when he first came to me for support. Not only was he struggling to cope professionally, but he had also lost his ability to function generally. He wasn't eating well, his new one-bedroom flat was empty but for a few necessary pieces of furniture, and his kitchen was full of unused appliances. Tom had also become socially withdrawn from his family, partner and friends. What emerged for Tom in his therapy was that he had never struggled in life.

> "I came from a wealthy family. I went to a top public school. I was bright. I had friends. I moved seamlessly through my education and into work. I have never known a time when who I was, was not enough. I have always been able to expand my capacity to cope and deal with life until now. Who I thought I was, is not who I now am. I thought I was my all-conquering-self fighting a battle I didn't know I was losing."
>
> Tom

Stages of Life FRGs can affect anyone at any time. They can occur in childhood or emerge later in adulthood. Critical to their formation are our expectations, often unconscious, regarding the new stage we are entering. It can be very easy to see new life stages as the continuation of old ones, bar the odd difference, and assume old identities and ways still apply. As Tom discovered, without high levels of self-awareness and adaptability, it can be easy for a Stages of Life FRG to form.

Stages of life FRGs I come across are those that occur during critical transitions, such as:

- primary to secondary school, secondary school to college, college to Further and Higher Education
- education into employment, employment into retirement
- career or role change, promotion into management and leadership, employment to self-employment, redundancy
- relationship stages and changes

  - single to partner, unmarried to married
  - child-free to parenthood
  - separation and divorce
  - old to new friendships

- relocation to a new area or country for personal or professional reasons.

Breaking it down, it often looks something like this:

- The Fantasy: someone believes, consciously or otherwise, that their old identities, behaviours and lifestyles will merge seamlessly with their new life stage
- The Reality: their existing identities, behaviours and lifestyles conflict with their new life stage.

General

General FRGs are based on the assumption that life will or should unfold in a 'general' way because of our individual, family and social backgrounds or other influences such as social media. This type of FRG swept my legs from under me a few years ago. I had assumed that financial wealth, professional status and the ability to provide a certain lifestyle for my children would all just fall into place. Looking back, this trajectory belonged to my father; it was his life. Although I knew this at some level—we took very different personal and professional journeys—it never occurred to me that I would not arrive at the same destination as my father. It was a house move that brought reality crashing in. Not only did I not have my father's wealth, for example, I didn't have any wealth at all. Although the period of depression that followed appeared to come out of nowhere, the truth was it had been building for some time.

My General FRG was principally financial and material, but they can relate to any area of life e.g., from relationships to careers and social status to our environment (where we work and live).

- The Fantasy: someone believes their life will or should follow a path that leads to general, desirable outcomes
- The Reality: only a proactive, flexible approach to life will create the desired outcomes.

Specific

In contrast to their General counterparts, Specific FRGs are born with the expectation that life will or should unfold in a 'specific' way'; when someone expects highly definable personal and professional outcomes to happen. A ridiculous example would be if I wished to score the winning goal for England in the next football World Cup Final. Often, though, specific outcomes start as entirely reasonable and realistic, like the desire to marry and have children, to become a doctor or earn a certain salary. What creates the Specific FRG is the failure to accept the moment when outcomes become unreasonable or unrealistic.

Despite their apparent differences, Specific FRGs form the same way as their General equivalents i.e., through individual, family, social or media influences, and can relate to any area of life.

- The Fantasy: someone believes life will or should follow a path that leads to specific, desirable outcomes
- The Reality: only a proactive, flexible approach to life will create specific outcomes.

The FRGs of others

Some FRGs, while impacting us individually, are really the creations of other people, usually those closest to us personally (parents, siblings, extended family and friends) and professionally (colleagues, bosses and professional peers). Intentionally or unintentionally, we can feel pressured by others into following a life path that reflects their values, beliefs and expectations rather than our own. When this is done with good, if misplaced intentions, we can willingly head down the path chosen for us because we trust the people concerned. However, if the intentions are less positive, we might do so out of fear. Children especially often do as they are told because they don't know any better and have a keen sense of what they stand to lose or gain e.g., parental approval or disapproval. You don't, though, have to be a child to create this type of FRG. Fear of disapproval and rejection, or the need for acceptance and validation, can apply equally to adults.

A defining characteristic of this FRG is the over or underestimation of an individual's abilities by others. I once worked with a young man in his early 20s whose low self-esteem and self-worth resulted in serial underachievement. I will never forget what he said in our first session. Even at primary school, he knew he would be the one who would not go to university. The explanation for this damaging self-assessment? His father had belittled him daily for as long as he could remember, creating the fantasy that he was no one and would achieve nothing. The Reality was he was someone who could accomplish a great deal (he is now a fully qualified accountant and volunteers for The Prince's Trust, mentoring disadvantaged young people).

Not all FRGs of Others form as above, however. Sometimes, they originate with the individual through a desire to positively or negatively impact another person in some way. A typical 'positive' example is when someone chooses an academic or professional path to improve the quality of someone else's life at their own expense. For example, as a university coach and therapist, I often met students studying to make their families proud, not themselves. The Fantasy here was the student believed university was the right choice and they should be capable of graduating. When they inevitably began to struggle under the strain of their FRG, they criticised themselves for failing instead of accepting the Reality that academic life was the problem, not themselves.

"I remember feeling electrified by the idea that I could choose my life rather than have it chosen for me. Mark pulled me out of my parent's life—studying to become a lawyer—and inserted me into my life. All I had ever wanted was to become a driving instructor. Don't ask me why, I just did. Making that call to my father to tell him I was leaving university to train as an instructor was the most exhilarating day of my life. My father told me not to bother coming home, and I said that was fine by me." Tariq

- The Fantasy – someone's identity, behaviours and lifestyle are the creation of others or are created for others
- The Reality – they have their own identity, behaviours and lifestyle, which they have the potential to create independently.

A means of escape

Human beings are a 'solution-orientated' species. Whenever we feel threatened, trapped or stuck, our instinct is to seek a way out of our predicament using whatever means we have at our disposal. Sometimes this works out well, and sometimes it doesn't. A Means Of Escape FRG is an example of when it doesn't.

Means Of Escape FRGs are created in response to adversity when, in an understandable desire to improve our life circumstances and chances, we lose sight of how to go about this realistically. The most common reasons I come across for why people create this type of unhelpful FRG are:

- low self-esteem
- trauma
- loss.

Take low self-esteem. People who don't value who they are, what they do and the life they lead can create Fantasy selves, behaviours and lifestyles as a means of escape because accepting and tackling their Reality is too hard or painful. A similar explanation lies at the heart of Means Of Escape FRGs born out of trauma or loss.

- The Fantasy – someone believes their identity, behaviours and lifestyle are a true reflection of who they are, what they do and the life they lead
- The Reality – their identity, behaviours and lifestyle are not a true reflection of who they are and are instead products of

adversity.

Plan A isn't working

When we like who we are, what we do, and the life we lead, we have what I call a Plan A. Plan As are great because the foundations, strategies and approaches upon which they are based make life much easier to navigate. However, like all good things, Plan As come with an Achilles Heel: they are the result, often over many years, of a lot of blood, sweat and tears. When, inevitably, the world changes around us, necessitating a Plan B, the sheer enormity of the effort required to develop it can often prove too much. Defeated, we fall back into the warm embrace of Plan A, which takes no effort at all. At that moment, when we double down on Plan A and ignore the evidence that it has stopped working, we create an unhelpful FRG by running our lives using a Plan that is out of sync with the world around us.

- The Fantasy – Plan A will come right eventually
- The Reality – Plan A will never come right, meaning Plan B is required.*

Stuck in the Fantasy: barriers to acceptance

Some people find acceptance easy to achieve and live with helpful FRGs, while others find it less straightforward. What follows are some barriers to acceptance I often encounter in my work.

A lack of awareness

In my introduction to unhelpful FRG types, I said that high levels of awareness can be noticeable by their absence, which is problematic because we can remain stuck in our fantasy without them. If we

---

* Plan Bs contain the best of Plan As without the worst of them alongside their own magic ingredients.

don't know something exists, how can we do something about it? Unfortunately, unhelpful FRGs do not come with flashing neon signs attached, nor do they send texts, emails or Direct Messages informing us of their presence, making them hard to spot.

I should add that being unaware is not a character flaw and something to be criticised for; we all go through periods when we are oblivious to things we need to know. Often the factors that create a lack of awareness, such as limited life experience or a poor support network, are rarely our fault alone. All we can do is adopt a position of kindness and compassion towards ourselves, combined with a sense of curiosity regarding what it is to thrive and survive and how to achieve it. This way, we can avoid beating ourselves up for lacking awareness and increase our chances of escaping its grip.

Luckily, though, most of us don't remain unaware indefinitely. While we might initially lack awareness of unhelpful FRGs at the level of thought and imagination, this rarely equates to no awareness at all. Remember the signs of unhelpful FRGs on pages 93 and 94. All of them are potential sources of awareness. They might not be neon signs, but they are doing the same job. We just have to recognise them for what they are, which, as I say, most of us get around to eventually because they are so unpleasant. For most of us, it is adversity that elevates our awareness of unhelpful FRGs to the necessary level of thought and imagination. Adversity serves to amplify the intensity of our negative signs until they provoke us into action—like talking to someone like me or picking up a book like this. Yes, we still need to join the dots by connecting our signs to unhelpful FRGs, but once fully aware, there is only one remaining barrier to overcome: letting go.

Letting go

Personal and professional experience tells me that most of us eventually get around to addressing our unhelpful FRGs, even if sometimes out of sheer necessity. Key to doing so successfully and at the least personal cost is letting go of our fantasy as painlessly as possible. The quicker and easier we can do so, the sooner we can embrace our reality and put our lives back on track.

However, while letting go is easy for some, it is difficult for others. Letting go means accepting who we have been, what we have been doing, and the life we have been leading have become the causes of our difficulties, not their solutions. Understandably, some can feel a level of resistance to or even fear at these unpalatable truths, but as the saying goes, 'resistance is futile'. When it comes to unhelpful FRGs, all resistance achieves is to make them bigger and more harmful.

When Adrian, a young man in his twenties, came to see me, he was severely depressed, experiencing suicidal thoughts and self-harming. Although we made some early progress, it was limited, and by our fourth session, he had relapsed. In seeking to make sense of his relapse, Adrian realised he was terrified of no longer being depressed. To him, being happy was an alien concept.

For all of his relatively young life, Adrian had mistaken his fantasy—his depressed self was his real self—for his reality. The possibility that the opposite was true shook him badly. "I thought I knew who I was. My fear was that I might glimpse happiness but fail to sustain it, and that terrified me more than staying depressed." Adrian had every reason to return to his fantasy state until I pointed out that it was the cause of the depression he had sought my help to lift. Faced with this undeniable logic, Adrian had no choice but to let go. All I had to do was demonstrate to Adrian that letting go could be a safe rather than frightening experience. When he saw that it could be, Adrian removed his final barrier to acceptance, enabling him to transform his unhelpful FRGs into helpful ones:

> "Mark helped me to realise the root cause of my problems and how to overcome them. Mark was able to offer a better perspective, which helped me to realise that things in my life were ultimately okay, but the way I was thinking and perceiving things in a negative way was keeping me in a depressed state.

Over the course of a few months, I started to perceive the world in a different way which led to a decrease in my depression, resulting in a genuine love for life again! I now have much more self-confidence, energy and motivation."
Adrian

So how did Adrian persuade himself to let go? He slowly, gently and sustainably experienced the benefits of going so.

The benefits of acceptance

As Damian, Tom and Adrian discovered, acceptance does not mean giving up and settling for a life of damage limitation. This is because:

'Acceptance is not resignation, but the first stage of transformation.'

Finding acceptance means we are no longer in conflict with our reality, which produces a range of benefits, including:

- Energy: being in conflict with our reality is highly energy intensive, the equivalent of rowing a boat with several holes in it. Finding acceptance means lost energy is returned to us to invest in getting our lives back on track.
- Confidence and motivation: with more energy, problem-solving and solution-finding become easier, resulting in increased confidence and motivation. Possibilities previously dismissed as too difficult become ones we want to act upon.
- Relationships: greater energy and confidence levels make it easier to ask for and receive support. Feeling like our 'old self' again changes how we relate to ourselves and those around us.
- Health and wellbeing: high energy levels, increased confidence and improved relationships all feed into our health and wellbeing. We sleep better and feel more motivated to do the basics, such as eating healthily and doing some exercise.
- Strengths and resources: finding acceptance reveals our

strengths and resources, which were hidden or warped in our fantasy state. And while these strengths and resources may be more or less than we imagined, because they are a true reflection, we no longer fall into the trap of under or overestimating what we are capable of.

Perhaps the most significant benefit, though, of acceptance is that it lays the foundations, in the form of helpful FRGs, for the successful progression through the final two stages of my IMPACT Model—Challenge and Transformation. Reaching these stages means we are really on our way to thriving and surviving.

Finding acceptance

Whether we are nudged, pushed or elbowed into finding acceptance, once we get a glimpse of it, as Adrian discovered, it can be hard to resist because of the possibilities it generates. So how do we find acceptance? Well, I hope this chapter helps you, of course, but there are sources all around us that can create the levels of awareness necessary for us to find acceptance. I have listed a few below, but there will be more.

- A coach or therapist.
- A self-help book or other media such as a podcast.
- A conversation (with impact).
- Adversity.
- Time, maturity, life experience.
- An event, incident or change of life circumstances.
- A memory.
- Boredom.
- Stories (films, books, plays etc.).

Living with acceptance and helpful FRGs

If who you are, is who you want to be, if what you are doing is what you want to be doing, and if how your life is, is how you want your life to be, then you will be fully thriving and surviving. Look at what happened to the lives of Damian, Tom and Adrian after they found acceptance and lived lives based on helpful FRGs. Damian graduated and is now pursuing a career in sports journalism. Tom settled happily into his medical career, married his partner and became the proud father of a little girl. And Adrian finished his engineering apprenticeship and started working for a Swiss engineering company.

Summary of Chapter Four:

- Unhelpful Fantasy-Reality Gaps capture the difference between what we think our current reality is and what it actually is. The bigger an unhelpful FRG, the more problematic it is.
- Closing unhelpful FRGs is essential for our thriving and surviving.
- Acceptance of our current reality is how we close unhelpful FRGs and transform them into helpful ones.
- There are different types of FRG and different causes of them.
- High levels of self-awareness are crucial for spotting and overcoming unhelpful FRGs
- Developing the ability to let go is critical
- Finding acceptance can be difficult, but achieving it comes with clear benefits.

THE TRIANGLE OF POSSIBILITY

The Triangle of Possibility

As human beings, we have no choice but to move forwards in time and space, meaning we have to move from a potentially infinite set of options to a single one. This is the decision-making process. I created my Triangle of Possibility to help people ensure their decision-making process is one that supports rather than undermines their thriving and surviving.

Along the bottom side of the triangle is the Line Where All Things Are Possible (LWATAP). Within the natural laws of the universe, any and every solution to our difficulties exist along our LWATAP. At the top is the Point Where Only One Thing Is Possible (PWOOTIP). Whenever we make a decision, big or small, we travel from our LWATAP to our PWOOTIP.

The aim is to be in control of this journey by travelling from the LWATAP along the sides of the triangle to a desirable PWOOTIP. The examples below are of undesirable PWOOTIP where control has been lost.

- Severe stress, anxiety and panic attacks, depression, anger.
- Addictions, compulsions and obsessions.
- Burnout, suicidal thoughts and actions, self-destruction.

Self-awareness and psychological flexibility are the tools we need to avoid ending up at harmful PWOOTIPs, such as those above. As we set off from our LWATAP towards our PWOOTIP, self-awareness allows us to tune into and observe the thoughts, behaviours and emotions we generate on our journey. Psychological flexibility enables us to make decisions based on our observations i.e., do we continue or turn around?

The good news is we have an ally on our journey, our Emotional Selves, who travel ahead of us to the likely PWOOTIP of our current journey. If our Emotional Selves like where we are headed, they will let us know by sending positive emotional messages, but if they don't, the message will be very different.

Difficult emotions are messages from our Emotional Selves telling us to turn around and head back to our LWATAP to regroup and begin a new journey. Encouraged by our Emotional Selves, our goal is for each new journey to last longer than before as we apply what we have learnt until one takes us all the way to a positive PWOOTIP. If we never or rarely reach positive PWOOTIPs, we know something needs to change.

Through self-awareness, psychological flexibility and support from our Emotional Selves, our Triangle of Possibility can end in 'growth, wellbeing and transformation'.

LWATAP: Line Where All Things Are Possible

PWOOTIP: Point Where Only One Thing Is Possible

C is for CHALLENGE

There isn't a living thing on the planet that isn't or shouldn't be engaged in the pursuit of thriving and surviving. However, fairly or unfairly, evolution has determined that achieving this optimum state requires continual investment. Put another way, being and staying alive is a Challenge, which is why it is a stage in my IMPACT Model.

Given that challenge is a 24/7 preoccupation, it is understandable that, as human beings, we represent what it means to us in a wide variety of ways. In my work as a coach and therapist, I am continuously amazed by the sources that inspire my clients to 'rise' to the challenges life throws at and presents to them. Do you recognise any of your challenges from the list below?

- Yourself.
- Significant people in their lives.
- Celebrities, influential people.
- Stories, literature, poetry.
- Film, theatre, television.
- Philosophy.
- The news.

- Social media.
- Education, academia.
- Professions and careers.

The good news is that evolution has equipped humans with the innate knowledge and ability to cope with challenge to maximise our chances of thriving and surviving. Our 'challenge' is to make that knowledge and ability work for us. A film that captures this beautifully is The Shawshank Redemption, which always crops up in my work. If you haven't seen it, then I highly recommend you do so, but if you have, you will know why Tony said the following:

"The film The Shawshank Redemption cropped up a lot talking to Mark. The final scene, when Tim Robbins is crawling through the sewer, knowing that at the end was his boat on the beach, was one we talked about as being symbolic of my relationship with challenge. The film really helped me befriend challenge when until then it had been my enemy." Tony

The nature of challenge
Challenge is good (most of the time)

Challenge is undoubtedly positive when it enables us to achieve personal, academic and professional transformation. In good times, challenge results in a sense of achievement, pride and satisfaction; in difficult times, it builds resilience and helps us feel secure.

Challenge is less positive when it exists in a form that prevents someone from progressing in life through no fault of their own, no matter how committed they are to overcoming it. Everything I write below, therefore, assumes that someone—maybe you—can overcome their challenges and achieve their Transformation even in the most difficult of circumstances.

Evolving challenge

Challenge is continuous, but how it presents itself will evolve as we journey through life. Challenge can be:

- predictable and unpredictable
- announced and unannounced
- short-lived and lifelong
- mental and physical
- internal (inside) and external (outside).

What most of us know is that the one constant of challenge is it is never the same.

Challenging language

If you were to describe who you are to yourself and others, what would you have to say on the subject of challenge? What language—words, phrases and imagery—would you use? For example, do you 'avoid' or 'embrace' challenge, 'welcome' or 'fear' it? Does your language express 'negativity' and 'self-doubt' or positivity and 'self-belief'? How would you answer if you were being interviewed for a job, for example, and were asked how you cope with challenge?

Our language can tell us a lot about our relationship with challenge. It sets the scene before a challenge is upon us, influences our progress as we go through it, and shapes our reflections once it has passed. If we want to make challenge work for rather than against us, we must use language that supports this goal, not undermines it. Use the box to record your initial observations about the language you do use.

Self-doubt	Self-belief

The emotions of challenge

The emotions of challenge can be positive and helpful, negative and unhelpful. Challenge can instil fear or excitement, dread or motivation, uncertainty or relief. Whatever emotions we feel, it is critical to remember the 'emotions as messages' idea I introduced in Chapter Two: that emotions are messages sent from our Emotional Selves. When it comes to challenge, emotions are, in effect, an assessment by our Emotional Selves about what it thinks our chances are of coming through it successfully. Positive emotions are a 'Thumbs Up!', negative emotions a 'Thumbs down!'

One source of information our Emotional Selves will draw upon in their assessment is what I call our 'history' of challenge. I will talk about this in more detail in the next section, but for now, consider this:

- if we have a 'negative' history of challenge i.e., we have a poor track record when it comes to overcoming or succeeding, our Emotional Selves will likely reflect this history in the emotional messages it sends.
- the opposite will be true if we have a positive history.

I like to imagine my Emotional Self pausing before it makes its mind up about which emotional message to send regarding my next challenge by asking me a series of questions about it.

- Have you been here before?
- Have you been here before and failed?
- If you failed, has anything changed since then?
- Have you been here before and succeeded?
- If you succeeded, is your approach still the right one, or does it need updating?
- Have you accurately assessed the level of challenge you face?
- Do you have the necessary resources and support in place?

No doubt your Emotional Self will ask you a different set of questions; however, rest assured it will take a close look at the answers you give, especially if they come in the form of silence. Remember, though, that your Emotional Self is on your side. It always wants to send you positive emotional messages, so tell them what they want to hear and reassure them with the answers you give.

A final thought on the emotions of challenge. When they are negative, such as fear, dread or apprehension, we mustn't misinterpret them as messages to give up. Instead, they are 99 times out of 100, encouraging us to return to the drawing board. In my experience, too many people throw the challenge-towel in when they experience anxiety-based emotions when what is required is not a change of challenge but a change of approach.

Your emotions of challenge	
Positive	Negative
•	•
•	•
•	•

A history of challenge

As I have suggested, when the next challenge comes along, our Emotional Selves will use the evidence we have supplied them (yes, this is what you have been doing) throughout our lives in determining which type of message to send. It will look back at our 'history of challenge'. What does challenge mean to us? Do we accept it as a part of life? Have we coped with it in a variety of forms? Have we been ready and prepared?

A positive history of challenge has the effect of diminishing the extent of each new challenge. We go into it equipped with what we need i.e., confidence, experience, knowledge and effective strategies, plus, critically, with the support of a contented Emotional Self. Conversely, a negative history has the effect of amplifying each new challenge as it comes along. We face our challenge ill-equipped, accompanied by an apprehensive Emotional Self.

Over time, we establish a 'baseline' of challenge, which our Emotional Selves use to assess new challenges. To judge which emotional messages to send, they use our history of challenge to evaluate if the latest challenge is:

- above, on, or below our baseline.
- beyond, on the limit of, or within our ability to deal with it.

Knowing our baseline is crucial, especially if forgetting it results in underestimating or overestimating ourselves. Many of us are great at embracing and coping with challenge; the trick is to remember we are! An obvious point, maybe, but time and again, I work with people who don't. Those who *don't* remember typically have low self-esteem and self-worth. Such traits make it hard to accept and recognise achievements and the pride and satisfaction that come with them. This is because doing so 'challenges' the negative view someone has of themselves. Forgetting resolves this conflict by hiding any successes where they won't be found, sometimes deleting them altogether.

> "Every time I said the next challenge was too great, I reconnected with my baseline and history of challenge. It was undeniable that I *did* challenge, and yet each time, I would forget. I was trapped in my house by anxiety. A year later, I graduated as a pharmacist. I changed my relationship with challenge, and that made the difference."
> David

In my experience, a positive history of challenge indicates an ability to: make hay while the sun shines and form a plan for when it (inevitably) stops.

A lesson in challenge: riding a bike.

In my work as a coach and therapist, clients often feel overwhelmed and defeated by the scale of their challenges. In such moments, I ask them whether they can ride a bike. Luckily, most can or remember learning.

"What happened when the stabilisers were taken off for the first time?" I ask.

The most common response is, "I wobbled and zigzagged for a few metres, fell off, and cried as blood poured from my grazed knees and elbows."

"At that moment," I continue, "did you decide that this whole biking thing wasn't for you?"

"No, of course not," comes the reply.

No, of course not. Instead of defeat, falling off simply made them more determined as they glimpsed the benefits of mastering this skill: freedom, prowess and roaming around with friends. The trouble with adults is they forget what their bike riding history has to tell them about their history of challenge. The failed New Year's Resolution is equivalent to a child falling off their bike and never getting back on again.

Entry Points

When we first imagine or are faced with a challenge, we can be 'challenged' in several ways, for example:

- it feels too big or difficult
- negative self-talk and defeatist language undermine our confidence and self-belief
- we decide it is too risky, for instance, in terms of time and money
- its future status creates too much uncertainty
- other people express their concerns and talk us out of trying.

No doubt there are other ways, but to get beyond these apparent 'truths' —which we must do if we are to make challenge a positive force in our lives—how we respond to the challenge we face is crucial. In 'The Emotions of challenge' on pages 120 and 121, I stated that whenever we feel emotionally defeated by a challenge, it is critical to remember that the feeling is rarely about the challenge itself and invariably about our strategy to achieve it.

One highly effective strategy to avoid falling at the first hurdle is to discover what I call our 'Entry Point', which is simply the point at which progress towards overcoming or succeeding at a challenge becomes possible. Entry Points are found by:

1. visualising an entire challenge through to completion
2. breaking it down into its constituent stages
3. using trial and error to find the stage where progress is possible
4. recognising...

    a. negative thoughts – "I knew I'd fail!"
    b. unhelpful behaviours – procrastination
    c. difficult emotions – anxiety, stress
       ... as valuable pieces of feedback that we have yet to

find our Entry Point and that further trial and error is required.

To illustrate my Entry Point idea, I will tell the story of Francesca, a university student I worked with. When she first came to see me, Francesca had not written a word of her final year dissertation for two months, meaning she was in real danger of failing her degree. Within seconds, tears were rolling down Francesca's face, and she was exhibiting signs of panic. Through gentle questioning, I learnt that her challenge was a seven-thousand-word dissertation on 'The History of the Corset' (Francesca was a fashion student).

Knowing that we had to find her Entry Point quickly, I sat Francesca down at my desk and asked her to go with my suggestion that she start typing words, any words, onto the blank computer screen in front of her.

"What should I type?"

"Anything."

After a few minutes, Francesca produced a short biography of herself.

"That's what I call your Entry Point," I said.

"What's that?" came the reply

"It's the point in any challenge where progress is possible. I guessed that your Entry Point was the act of writing itself because you haven't written anything for two months. I needed to find out where you *could* start."

A nod of understanding.

"Can you write me a sentence about the corset? Anything—when it was invented, what it's made of etc."

Francesca thinks and then types. Prompted by my use of 'Who, what, where, when, why and how' questions, she produced a detailed outline of her dissertation.

"That's more than I've written in two months," she said. "I don't understand why it was so easy."

"No?"

"Because I didn't know my Entry Point?"

I nod. "I broke your challenge into its individual stages, with the first being typing out words. I saw that this calmed you down, so I nudged you into typing words about corsets, then sentences. Did you notice that I said nothing for the last fifteen minutes, and you just typed?"

"No, I didn't! Oh my god!"

When Francesca discovered that her initial overwhelm and paralysis were instructions to find her Entry Point and not to give up, she made progress. So, if you feel defeated by a challenge, remember to find your Entry Point:

- if a challenge feels too big, break it down
- treat negative thoughts, behaviours and emotions as valuable pieces of feedback
- think about time and money blocks as forms of avoidance, which self-belief and backing yourself can remove
- avoid the certainty trap i.e., the need to see a clear outcome before commencing your journey. Few challenges would ever be achieved if it were necessary to know the end before the beginning
- if others don't believe in you, find someone new to talk to, someone who can give you a Conversation With Impact.

"I had lived in Spain for eight years but never learnt to speak Spanish. The fear of failure was so intense. My wife was Spanish, but my fear just made us fall out whenever she tried to teach me, so we gave up. Mark suggested his entry point idea, and bingo. I downloaded a language app, found myself an online tutor in England! And then negotiated lessons with my wife. Looking back, the challenge felt too enormous when in reality, it wasn't. I will never forget the day I bought a bus ticket and ordered a meal in Spanish. I didn't fail, and no one laughed at me."

Lee

The challenge paradox

My Entry Point idea is connected to another that I call The Challenge Paradox. As a practitioner, I work on the assumption that if someone could overcome their challenges by themselves (and with their existing support network), they would do so. If they can't, it means they have either too little or too much challenge in their life, creating the following double-bind: the inability to make progress while recognising that progress is necessary. It is this predicament I call The Challenge Paradox.

The Challenge Paradox is my term, of course, but my guess is that you will have your own. Recognise any of these?

- Stuck
- paralysed
- blocked
- trapped
- imprisoned.

So many of us remain 'trapped' in The Challenge Paradox because it feels inescapable. No matter which way we turn, no matter what we try, we keep returning to the same point. Exhausted and demoralised, we give up. However, it doesn't have to be this way.

Matthew was at a very low ebb when he came to see me and on a wild goose chase in search of happiness. After another outburst of anger at his wife, she told him straight that he either sorted things out or their marriage was over. At that moment, Matthew felt at his lowest. How could he promise his wife he would sort something he had failed to sort for years? He even started to believe that splitting up was the answer. The Challenge Paradox changed all that. I helped Matthew realise he didn't know what his challenge was, which explained why he never got anywhere. He thought it was his anger when it was his family, specifically his parents and brother. Matthew's family were toxic, but his approach had been to win them around and make excuses for them.

I suggested that Matthew use the next time they disrespected him or his family to trigger his Entry Point, which for him was sending an honest email. He didn't have to wait long. His brother insulted his wife over something small, allowing Matthew to email his family how he saw things. Needless to say, they didn't reply. Since then, Matthew has had no contact with his sibling and has a transactional relationship with his parents. Guess what? He is happy. His wife says she has her husband back and his daughter, her father back.

We must realise, as Matthew did, that being trapped in The Challenge Paradox does not indicate we are incapable of progress; it means we have yet to make the concept of challenge work for us. And as I have suggested, one of the most effective ways to achieve this is to find our Entry Point—once we know what our challenge is, of course.

The challenge of good ideas

There is nothing like a good idea, one that suggests a resolution to our difficulties. As you might expect, Emotional Selves love good ideas, too, because they offer the prospect of us getting our thriving and surviving back on track or keeping it so. With the possibility of change in the air, Emotional Selves switch to states of curiosity and anticipation instead of worry and concern. In the immediate aftermath of our good idea, Emotional Selves look kindly upon us, allowing us a honeymoon period. However, there is a harsh reality to new ideas. If our Emotional Selves do not see a ripple effect of change flowing from them, they can quickly conclude that our new idea is just that—an idea—and respond in the only way they know how: by sending appropriate emotional messages in the form of difficult emotions. Roughly translated, these messages would read something like this:

"What are you playing at?"

"What happened to your good idea?"

"This was supposed to be when you got yourself back on track. Now what?"

Emotional Selves don't care that good ideas are sometimes easier to think up than implement. All they know is that it doesn't make sense to leave a good idea gathering dust on our mental drawing boards. This, therefore, is the 'challenge' of new ideas. Once we have them, we need to act soon to reassure our Emotional Selves that we aren't just talking a good game.

The Goldilocks Principle of Challenge: not too little, not too much, but just right

My goal as a practitioner is always to find ways of communicating my concepts in understandable ways. My Goldilocks Principle of Challenge has proven to be one of my most popular. Borrowed from the famous fairy tale of Goldilocks and the Three Bears, The Goldilocks Principle helps people establish an optimum level of challenge: not too little, not too much, but just right. Most of us progress with our challenges in a 'higgledy-piggledy' fashion in that we have good and not-so-good days. The critical aspect is that despite any setbacks, we are moving forwards. If we are, we are making The Goldilocks Principle work, but if we aren't, then we're not. Establishing an optimum level of challenge is not an exact science but a process of trial and error, which Goldilocks' porridge-tasting mirrors. In the original story, Goldilocks tries all three bowls of porridge before settling on Baby Bear's because it is 'just right'. Like the eponymous little girl of the fairy tale, as long as we persevere, trying this and trying that, we stand a good chance of overcoming or achieving our challenge.

The right challenge but the wrong strategy

Many people find it easy to identify the challenge they face or choose a challenge to set themselves, but then become stuck. One common explanation for grinding to a halt with a challenge is when we have: the right challenge but the wrong strategy. As one client memorably said to me once:

"I was aiming for a summit sat on top of a different mountain to the one I was climbing."

Too often, we misinterpret failures to overcome or achieve challenges as evidence that they are beyond us, i.e., they are too challenging. My 'right challenge but the wrong strategy' idea offers a kinder and potentially more accurate interpretation: the challenge is not the problem; it's the strategy to achieve it that needs attention. So, instead of giving up on losing weight, finding a new job, or ending a relationship, the focus shifts to changing the 'how' —the strategy—until it realigns with the challenge. For example:

- someone struggling to lose weight might:
    o   replace exercising alone with exercising with others
    o   supplement exercise with weight loss medication
    o   focus equally on diet, nutrition and exercise
    o   use life coaching and hypnotherapy alongside other approaches

- someone struggling to find a new job might:
    o   work with a careers consultant instead of by themselves
    o   update their skills and training before applying
    o   develop their interview skills rather than rely on old approaches
    o   get a C.V. specialist to update their C.V. to ensure it shows them in the best possible light

- someone struggling to end a relationship might:
    o   work with a life coach instead of being supported by friends
    o   focus on building their self-esteem and assertiveness first
    o   use therapy to explore their poor relationships patterns
    o   suggest couples therapy to their partner as a way to end as positively as possible.

Some challenges are too important to be abandoned because of their significance for our personal and professional circumstances, but give up on them people do. By making strategy the focus, challenges become possible as the penny drops that they were never the problem in the first place. And while there might be only one example of a challenge e.g., changing careers, there will be many strategies to achieve it, which increases confidence in successful outcomes.

Types of challenge

How we tackle challenges will depend on their type. For example, does a challenge concern us alone, or does it involve others? Is it a challenge of our own making or choosing, or can responsibility be handed to someone else? Over the following few pages, I look at different types of challenges to help you better understand your own. Correct 'diagnosis' of the kind of challenge we face allows for effective and efficient targeting of resources, saving us precious time, energy and money.

Internal and external challenges

Common internal challenges include:

- poor mental and physical health
- poor overall wellbeing
- negative thinking styles, negative mindset
- negative, self-limiting beliefs
- self-sabotaging behaviours e.g., perfectionism
- psychological inflexibility
- difficult emotional states e.g., anxiety or depression
- poor sense of identity or self
- low self-esteem and self-worth
- low self-confidence
- traumatic memories and past experiences.

I wonder what you think about this type of challenge? Had it occurred to you, for example, that low self-esteem was a type of challenge or psychological inflexibility? In my experience, challenge is often perceived as an external rather than internal experience, which is problematic for accurate diagnosis. What can prevent us from falling into this trap is the definition of challenge we use. For me, a challenge is anything that impedes our ability to thrive and survive, including ones external to us and internal. I would suggest this is a far more helpful definition, as it means we don't disregard 50% of what might be standing in our way.

Common external challenges include:

- people, relationships and support in personal and professional contexts
- organisations and services we use and rely on
- a lack of information and knowledge, or the wrong type
- a lack of resources, or the wrong type
- organisational factors e.g., stressful or toxic workplaces
- environmental factors e.g., expensive commutes
- social and cultural factors e.g., gender, ethnicity & sexuality bias.

Internal and external challenges can and often do overlap and influence each other, of course. For example, when an employee experiences mental health issues (internal) due to bullying at work (external) or when low self-esteem (internal) results in people-pleasing relationships (external), or when trauma (internal) results in abusive relationships (external).

> "It reached the stage where I could not be alone because I was too anxious. I saw a hypnotherapist because I thought the challenge was my work, specifically my fear of public speaking. Deal with that, I thought, and my anxiety would go away. It was only when I realised the challenge was my non-existent self-esteem and not meetings at work that I began to make progress."
> Patricia

Misdiagnosing internal and external challenges is easily done, as Patricia discovered. So how can you be precise? As I have suggested, having a better definition of challenge can help, but using my 'emotions as messages' idea is another way. If you remain stressed or anxious, for example, in your attempts to address your challenges, you know your Emotional Self is unconvinced by your diagnostic powers. The message here is, "Return to your lists of internal and external challenges and take another, closer look."

Individual (self-imposed), collective (imposed by others)

When someone comes to see me for help with a challenge, I am keen to establish its individual or collective origin i.e., who is responsible. Some examples are clear-cut, for example:

- a student who chooses to study for a degree takes individual responsibility for the challenge of graduating
- a couple who wants to improve their lifestyle is taking collective responsibility for eating more healthily, earning more money, and improving their work/life balance.

In these instances, it is clear who has responsibility; however, this is not always the case. For example, when an individual has to tackle a challenge created by others or when others have to face one imposed by an individual, such as:

- a student whose parents choose a different degree for them to study than they would have chosen for themselves
- a couple who seeks to improve their lifestyle to cope with work-related stress caused by a demanding, inflexible employer.

Correctly identifying the source of a challenge is vital for meaningful progress. If it belongs to you, no one else can overcome it for you; if it belongs to someone else, you can't solve it for them. There is something objectionable when an individual abdicates their responsibility or takes responsibility for a challenge set by others. And yet, due to poor self-awareness, misguided loyalties or coercion, this does happen. So, taking my student examples:

- honesty and acceptance remove the inner conflict caused by personal abdication e.g., "I choose to go to university. My parents didn't force me. It's down to me to turn things around."
- Additional burdens can be lifted when responsibility is correctly allocated, such as self-blame for struggling with a challenge, e.g., "My parents are responsible, not me. They need to acknowledge this."
- The ownership of the challenge can be switched e.g., "I'll take the degree chosen for me, but I'll use it to find work that takes me away from my parents."
- Choices and options become available e.g., "Now I know misguided loyalty to my parents was the issue, I can switch degrees or leave university to pursue my own academic and professional paths."*

Events

Tom stares back at me with the look of someone who is not in good shape. A former soldier in the British Army, Tom has come to see me for Post-Traumatic Stress Disorder. Although he had been in many traumatic situations, Tom explained his trauma in specific terms. At the last minute, a close friend took his place on a routine patrol (they were stationed in Afghanistan) and was killed by a roadside bomb. Tom blamed himself and could not shake the belief that he should have been killed, not his friend.

Tom's challenge—PTSD—was caused by an event, my third type of challenge, when life becomes more challenging because

---

* A footnote: all of the examples are true. Take it from me, if you want to avoid burning yourself out tackling a challenge, make sure you know which of these types it is.

of something that directly or indirectly happens to us. Event types are similar to Individual and Collective Challenges in that correctly assigning responsibility for them is critical for a successful resolution. Central to Tom's recovery was his willingness to accept that he wasn't to blame. He was initially vehemently opposed to any suggestion that he wasn't culpable until I pointed out his heartfelt, if incorrect, belief was maintaining his trauma. Coming to see me, I said, conflicted with his determination to blame himself for the death of his friend. After that conversation, Tom made good progress.

Another client, Trisha, provided an opposite example. She came for coaching and therapy after her husband left her for being unfaithful. Trisha fully accepted she was at fault, which made it easier to help her achieve the challenge of getting her life back on track.

Common events-related challenges include those related to the following:

- work e.g., redundancy, dismissal, company relocation
- relationships e.g., separation and divorce
- family e.g., bereavement, life setbacks for children
- illness to self or others
- trauma e.g., road traffic accidents, assault
- finances e.g., debt caused by a change in life circumstances
- environmental e.g., homelessness.

Ongoing and specific

Specific challenges have a start, middle and end, whereas ongoing ones have no end in sight. A three-year degree course is a specific challenge, and caring for someone with a chronic health condition is ongoing.

Whether by accident or design, many of us are adept at turning specific challenges into ongoing ones, such as staying in an unhappy job or relationship rather than leaving them. Sometimes the two types merge together. Perfectionists, for example, present an ongoing challenge to themselves in their never-ending search for the perfect self, achievement or lifestyle based on a series of specific challenges, such as body augmentation, DIY projects or personal and professional status.

Past, present and future

Finally, challenges can be seen in terms of the past, present and future. Past challenges include being raised in difficult circumstances or being impacted by past adverse events. Present challenges include those resulting from change and upheaval in our personal and professional lives, such as divorce and redundancy, and those characteristic of key life stages, such as parenthood. And future challenges include those that require anticipating and planning for, such as career changes and retirement. There is often overlap, of course, such as when past challenges create present and future ones or when future challenges lead to ones in the present.

Your challenges

Irrespective of the type of challenge we face, they all have one thing in common: they need addressing, and in this section, I turn my attention to helping you address your challenges. By the end of this section, you will be in a position to:

- identify your priority areas of challenge
- understand who you need to be and what you need to do to tackle your challenges successfully
- recognise and find the resources you need to deal with your challenges.

C IS FOR CHALLENGE

As a reminder, below are the areas featured throughout this book where all our challenges will be located. To get you started, enter as much information into the table as possible about your current knowledge and understanding of your challenges, and then complete my 0–10 Challenge activity.

Area of challenge	Type of Challenge	Important or unimportant
- Yourself: identity, role and status; self-esteem and self-worth		
- Home and family life		
- Relationships – personal and professional		
- Work, career and professional development		
- Health and wellbeing		
- Financial		
- Lifestyle		
- Social		
- Cultural		
- Environment		
- Past, present and future		

THE 0-10 CHALLENGE

The 0–10 Challenge

Step 1 – identifying your priority and non-priority areas of challenge.* Using a 0–10 scale (0=an area in great shape, 10=an area in very poor shape), choose numbers that capture the scale of your challenge in each area. As a general rule:

- Scores of 7 or more indicate areas of severe or very severe challenge that need tackling as a matter of priority
- Scores of 5 or 6 indicate areas of mild-to-moderate challenge that need tackling soon
- Scores of 4 or below indicate areas of little-to-no challenge that can be tackled once priority areas have been addressed or even left alone entirely.

What did you discover? Did the exercise confirm what you already know, or did it throw up some surprises?

Step 2 – establishing your present and future positions. I have suggested throughout this chapter that making challenge work for rather than against us happens when our identity and behaviours are in good shape and harmony with each other. In facing up to or embarking on our next challenge, we must understand the degree to which they are or are not if we are to make good, sustained progress.

Taking your priority areas of challenge identified in Step 1, choose two numbers between 0 and 10 that indicate where you are now (Point A) and where you need to be (Point B), and reflect on the following questions:

Who:

- Who are you at Point A? For example, "I am at 3/10 because I am too unconfident."

---

* If we don't prioritise then everything becomes as important as everything else, which is a sure-fire way to burning out and undermining our ability to thrive and survive. Emotional Selves need us to prioritise and take a dim view of when we don't.

- Who will you be at point B? For example, "I am at 8/10 because I am full of confidence."
- Who do I need to be to get from Point A to Point B? For example, "I need to be brave and committed."

What:

- What are you doing at Point A? For example, "I am at 3/10 because I am avoiding and procrastinating."
- What are you doing at Point B? For example, "I am at 8/10 because I am proactive and productive."
- What do you need to do to get from Point A to Point B? For example, "I need to find my Entry Point and take baby steps."

How did you find completing Steps 1 and 2? It would be expected if you found them challenging, so be kind to yourself. Please recognise that you are at the start of a process, and avoid criticising yourself for not being at the end of it.

Step 3 – The Challenge Audit. If there is one idea I would like you to brand deeply into your brain, it is this:

- too little or too much challenge is always a matter of resources, and that we don't have enough of what we need.

For me, this idea is powerful and liberating because it suggests that in the majority of cases—there will always be exceptions—too little or too much challenge is not a fixed state we are powerless to affect, but one we can change for the better. Too many people are passive in the face of challenge, assuming it will always be their enemy. My Challenge Audit is designed to 'challenge' this belief by helping you discover what resources you have in sufficient quantities and what you need to find more of.

So, what do I mean by a 'resource'? I mean anything that can transform levels of challenge from unhelpful to helpful. A resource can be both internal e.g., self-esteem, or external e.g., people. There are no right or wrong combinations, only what we need for the challenge we face.

Reflecting on your outcomes from Steps 1 and 2, look at the nine boxes below, which contain the range of resources I think we need to have a positive relationship with challenge. Again, using a 0–10 scale, choose a number representing how much or how little each resource you possess. As a rule:

- scores of 7 or above indicate a resource you don't have enough of that you will need to find more of as a matter of urgency
- scores of 5 or 6 indicate a resource you have enough of to help you tread water but which you will need to find more of soon
- scores of 4 or below indicate a resource you have enough or more than enough of that you need to nurture and protect.

INFORMATION, TECHNOLOGY, KNOWLEDGE	SKILLS & ABILITIES	CONFIDENCE & BELIEF
WELLBEING	SUPPORT	MOTIVATION
TIME	ENVIRONMENT	STRATEGY

With your scores in mind, consider the following questions:

- INFORMATION, TECHNOLOGY, KNOWLEDGE: Do I have enough of these? If I don't, can I find them myself, or does someone else have what I need?
- SKILLS & ABILITIES: Do I have what is required? If I don't, can I develop them independently, or will I need support?
- CONFIDENCE & BELIEF: Do I have enough? If I don't, can I build these qualities on my own, or will I need the backing of others?

- WELLBEING: Do I feel resilient enough? If I don't, can I increase my resilience by myself, or will I need encouragement?
- SUPPORT: Do I have enough around me? If I don't, where will I find what I need, and who will provide it?
- MOTIVATION: Do I feel sufficiently energised? If I don't, can I galvanise myself, or will I need inspiration from others?
- TIME: Do I have enough spare capacity? If I don't, can I create it individually, or will I need to collaborate?
- ENVIRONMENT: Am I in the right environment? If I'm not, can I change my existing surroundings, or do I need to be somewhere else?
- STRATEGY: Do I have the right strategy? If I don't, how will I acquire it? On my own or through co-operation.

What did you discover about the current state of your resources? Did your scores and answers confirm what you already know, or did they surprise you? Can you make sense of your current level of challenge, whether it is too high, too low or just right? And does your present rate of progress in overcoming or achieving your latest challenge also make sense to you? Whatever you discovered, I hope you are in a better position to identify what resources you need, where and how to find them.

> "My problems started when I was unexpectedly made redundant. I was not in a good place for a long time. Listing all of my challenges, it quickly became evident that I saw every challenge as equally important. No wonder I was overwhelmed. Prioritising my challenges down to a manageable number gave me the headspace I needed to see that who I was, was the problem. I knew how to get a new job, but redundancy had shattered my sense of self. The 0–10 Challenge reconnected who I was to what I knew and gave me the resources I needed to brave the job market again."
> Sally

C IS FOR CHALLENGE

THE STRETCH ZONE

The Stretch Zone

The final concept of the Challenge stage is the Stretch Zone, a well-known model that beautifully captures how to safely and sustainably approach your challenges. The Stretch Zone is made up of three circles.

- The inner circle represents your Comfort Zone. Do not be misled by the name. Your Comfort Zone is where you are trying to escape from. It is where you hide away from the challenges that scare you and for which you feel ill-equipped.
- The middle circle is called your Stretch Zone. This is where you are trying to get to because it is a place of growth and transformation. Stretch Zones are not, by design, comfortable to be in but are intended as personal or professional spaces you can adapt to through courage and commitment.
- The third circle is aptly named your Panic Zone. Anyone who spends most of their time in their Comfort Zone will know this place well, as it is where they keep stepping into in their unsuccessful attempts at transformation.

The aim is to step into your Stretch Zone by setting challenges that, while 'stretching', are not so demanding that they trigger panic in you. What you are trying to avoid is stepping out of your Comfort Zone and straight into your Panic Zone by placing the bar too high for yourself, i.e., setting challenges that are beyond you. Panic Zones explain themselves.

How do you know if you are finding your Stretch Zone? Because you won't be frantically trying to escape from it in search of the warm embrace of your Comfort Zone. You will feel a level of discomfort in your Stretch Zone, but it is the type that readily transforms itself into a sense of accomplishment when you dig deep and refuse the lure of your Comfort Zone. Emotional Selves love Stretch Zones because they are where we learn the knowledge and develop the skills to thrive and survive.

The goal is to spend more and more time in your Stretch Zone through trial and error. Learn what trials and tests provide the right level of challenge and how to increase those levels incrementally. Importantly, hang in there because the magic starts when you get it right. The more time you spend in your Stretch Zone, the bigger it gets. And the bigger it gets, the smaller the other two Zones become. You may still spend some time in your Comfort or Panic Zones, but no more than anyone else.

Summary of Chapter Five

- Challenge is a part of life, and as human beings, we represent it in many ways and forms.
- We have our own relationship with challenge that can be understood in terms of language, emotions and history.
- Making progress with our challenges requires breaking them down, finding our Entry Point and aligning our challanges and strategies.
- Challenge can be paradoxical.
- To make challenge work for rather than against us, we need to apply The Goldilocks Principle of Challenge: not too little, not too much, but right.
- There are different types of challenge, which we must correctly identify to make progress.
- Overcoming and achieving our challenges requires that we know:
    - how to prioritise them in order of importance
    - who we need to be and what we need to do
    - the current state of our resources and whether we have enough of what we need.

T is for TRANSFORMATION

Over the last five chapters, I have asked you to consider how to thrive and survive from the perspective of:

- Impact
- Meaning
- Patterns
- Acceptance
- Challenge.

In this chapter, I look at the concept of Transformation, the sixth and final stage. Whether we move swiftly or methodically through the six stages of The IMPACT Model, the final stage of Transformation is the one we all wish to reach and journey beyond because it is then that we will be:

- who we want to be
- doing what we want to do
- living the life we want to live.

A journey and a destination

Fundamental to my approach is the idea that transformation is both a journey and a destination. The journey consists of the individual steps we take; the destination where we want those steps to take us. To thrive and survive, we must ensure our journey and destination are connected. When we run into trouble, it is when:

- we have no journey to start or desired destination to head for
- we are on the wrong journey for our desired destination
- we are on the right journey for our desired destination but lack the means to complete it.

Clearly, we will go on many journeys and reach many destinations during our lives. As you work through this chapter, you might find it helpful to focus on your current journey and destination; look back at a past journey and destination to consider what, if anything, you would change; or 'travel' to a future journey and destination to plan for them.

> "I thought there was a perfect destination waiting for me. All I had to do was find it. I searched and searched for my destination in each new relationship, house move, possession, job, but I was completely ignoring my journey. Learning that the journey helps create the destination was a huge thing for me. It helped me to notice the beauty around me, and to be more appreciative of the moment. I did eventually arrive at my destination, but it was not what I expected. It was made up of everything I encountered along the way."
> Saskia

Later, you will get the opportunity to map out some ideal journeys and destinations, but for now, a question for you to ponder: is your transformation on track or not?

Kickstarting your transformation

> "No problem can be solved from the same level of consciousness that created it."
> Einstein

When our attempts at transforming ourselves and our situation plateau or go into reverse, we know two things: we don't have a clear idea of what we are transforming or how to go about it. Taking Einstein's quote, we are trying to find solutions from a problem-generating level of consciousness. Ever thought you were getting somewhere digging that hole? This chapter aims to shift you into a solution-generating level of consciousness. How this happens is less important than that it does, but one very effective way is storytelling. A few years ago, I wrote the story below to kickstart a client's transformation after they became stuck and I became stuck helping them. It had the desired effect.

Manhole Cover

A man walks out of his front door and immediately falls down an open manhole that lies right outside. To the casual observer, this looks like an unfortunate accident, but what about the man's friends, family and neighbours? What do they think? What conclusions do they draw? To them, there was nothing accidental or unfortunate about the man's sudden disappearance because they knew this deep and toxic hazard was there before the man left his house. How did they know? Because it has been there for some time. The man knew, too, of course. He knew when he woke up, brushed his teeth and ate his breakfast. And yet that day, just like the many days before, down he went into the grime and the filth of the sewer below. So, far from being accidental, the man's daily fate seems preordained somehow. Is it deliberate? An act of self-punishment, maybe? The truth is that no one really knows, not even the man himself. What might surprise anyone reading this story who doesn't know the man, is the number of times he has fallen down the manhole. Actually, no one knows the exact number because they stopped counting a long time ago. Let's just say the number is a big one. How does he keep doing something so demonstrably harmful when the solution seems so obvious? Why doesn't the penny drop? Why doesn't he cover the hole with a manhole cover? You would, wouldn't you?

I'll admit Manhole Cover is perhaps not my best story, but reading it proved to be a turning point for my client. It helped him see where and how he was going wrong, kickstarting his transformation. Of course, stories aren't the only way. Others include:

- a coach or therapist
- a self-help book
- a conversation (with impact)
- adversity
- time, maturity, life experience
- an event, incident or change of life circumstances
- a memory
- boredom
- stories (films, books, plays etc.).

Transformation: who, what, where, when, why and how

To progress on our journey towards our destination, we need to know exactly what we are transforming, which for me, breaks down neatly into the following categories.

- Who – in addition to ourselves, there will be those that are transformed by our transformation, people we know personally and professionally, plus those involved in it.
- What – this is a broad category that I break down into our internal and external realities. The lists in the box are not exhaustive, so if you think of more, please add them.

T IS FOR TRANSFORMATION

Internal reality	External reality
- Identity, role and status (personal and professional)	- Identity, role and status (personal and professional)
- Thoughts, behaviours and emotions	- Home and family
- Self-talk, inner dialogue	- Wider personal and professional support networks and the conversations we have with them
- Relationships with, beliefs about and perceptions of the external world (people, places and 'stuff')	
- Mental, physical and psychological health and wellbeing	- Academic and professional qualifications, skills, training, knowledge and experience
- Past, present and future focus and attention	- Lifestyle
	- Social and cultural factors
- Memories	- Environment
- Sensory experiences and phenomena	- The relationship the external world has with us and how it perceives who we are, what we do and the life we lead
- Skills and abilities, strengths and resources	
- Our values i.e., what is important to us	- Work, job, career, employer, sector
- Social and cultural influences	

- Where – transformation can happen inside and outside of us and at home, at work, and in the social spaces we spend time in.
- When – transformation can happen at any time, of course, but commonly when it is in response to adversity, triggered by personal and professional development, and when we transition between significant life stages, such as education into work, single to shared lives.
- Why – sometimes because we want to transform ourselves

and our lives, and sometimes because we have to. The context of our lives can determine the 'why', such as a desire to achieve specific outcomes or overcome adversity.
- How – transformation can be a solo or collective endeavour with minimal or significant resourcing. It can be structured and deliberate or allowed to occur more freely.

Attention and transformation

As human beings, we have no choice but to move forwards in time and space, otherwise known as the ageing process. This means we are on a journey of transformation, heading towards a destination of transformation whether we like it or not. Now, I don't know about you, but this is one process I want to be in control of as much as possible.

The importance of the ideas involved here cannot be understated. As we journey through life toward our various destinations, our mind/body systems take the 'material' we gather and produce along the way and literally build our journey of transformation with it. Where we focus our attention, what on and why is crucial in determining whether the material we acquire and generate is, in simple terms, positive or negative. By material, I am referring to things like our thoughts, behaviours and emotions, and outcomes from our interaction with the world we inhabit. And here is the critical idea to understand:

Because our mind/body systems operate to some degree independently of us, it means our transformation is partly out of our hands.

When our attention is positively focused and the material, we give our mind/body systems equally so, this 'independence' can be a great thing, like someone else doing much of the hard work of transformation for us. However, when our attention is negatively focused and the material harmful, the autonomy of our mind/body systems can be anything but great. The 'trouble' with our mind/body systems is they can be very obedient and work uncritically with the material we give them. If the material is negative, they just shrug their shoulders and get on with it. They don't want to, but in the absence of any positive material to work with, our mind/body systems are left with no choice but to use what is available. Why? Because they have to move us forwards in time and space.

Damian

Remember Damian, the 'lazy', 'marijuana smoking' university student I introduced you to in Chapter Four on Acceptance? Because of low self-esteem, trauma and poor mental health, his attention was focused on:

- his perceived inadequacies as a student
- the likelihood of academic failure in the final year of his degree
- acquiring drugs
- spending time with friends who didn't care about their degrees either
- handling his parents when they found out he had failed his degree.

Consequently, Damian was generating *a lot* of negative material for his mind/body system to work with. The result? His transformation was completely off-track because he was on a journey taking him away from his desired destination, not towards it. This is why it is so important for us to know how to generate positive material and the role attention plays in this. Without this knowledge, our mind/body systems cannot play their part in getting us to where we want to be as enjoyably and rewardingly as possible.

Some principal drivers of negatively focused attention and the generation of negative material include:

- difficult childhoods

- poor mental health
- identity issues
- low self-esteem, self-worth and confidence
- limiting beliefs
- problematic, toxic and abusive relationships
- trauma
- harmful and destructive lifestyles
- challenging personal and professional circumstances.

To succeed in our transformation, we need to know if any of the above are influential in our lives so we can do something about them. Remember what happened to Damian. He got his degree back on track, graduated and began his career in journalism when he focused his attention on who he wanted to be, what he wanted to do and the life he wanted to live.

Activity: what type of material are you producing?

Material	Positive	Negative
Thoughts		
Behaviours (actions)		
Emotions/feelings		
Outcomes from interactions and relationships (with yourself and the outside world: people, places and 'stuff')		

T IS FOR TRANSFORMATION

A journey through time

It is one thing to know we are on a journey of transformation, headed for a destination of transformation, but another to know where we are at any given time on our journey and in relation to our destination. Understanding these 'reference points' is vital if we are to avoid losing our way. I like to check where I am, both daily and across extended periods, by asking myself the following questions:

- is today going to be like yesterday? (daily reference check)
- is my past, present and future in harmony? (extended period check)

Actually, another reason I ask myself these questions is that even if I don't, someone else will. Who? I hear you ask—my Emotional Self, who asks these questions as part of its ongoing monitoring and assessment of my thriving and surviving. It asks them in expectation of convincing answers because it wants to know from me that my transformation—a crucial part of my thriving and surviving—is on track. And because you have an Emotional Self, you are being asked these questions, too. Rest assured, Emotional Selves will have their own view of the current state of our transformation. So if our answers are at odds with it or are unconvincing, they will respond by sending emotional messages in the form of stress or anxiety. So what answers do we need to give to get our Emotional Selves onside?

Is today going to be like yesterday?

If yesterday was a good day, our answer needs to be, "Yes, today will be like yesterday. More of the same." However, if yesterday was not a good day, then our answer needs to be, "No, today won't be like yesterday, and this is how I will be turning things around." Our Emotional Selves love these answers because it reassures them that we know how to keep our transformation on track through good days and bad. What they don't love is either silence because we don't know the question is being asked in the first place or answers that indicate we don't know how to:

- keep the good days going
- turn the bad days around.

Is my past, present and future in harmony?

The types of answers our Emotional Selves love to receive to this question might go something like this:

- "I will take into my present what has worked in the past and leave behind what hasn't."
- "I will maintain and improve what is working in the present and address what isn't."
- "I will grow and nurture the potential emerging in my present and take it into my future."
- "I have a positive vision for my future that my past and present will help me to achieve."

Similarly, a dim view is taken by Emotional Selves to silence or 'don't know how' for this question, too.

Harmony and consistency

The aim is to ensure harmony and consistency between 'today and yesterday' and between our 'past, present and future'. Harmony and consistency reassure and inspire our Emotional Selves, giving them confidence that our transformation is on track. Disharmony and inconsistency ring alarm bells:

- How can today be an improvement on yesterday if we don't know why yesterday was a 'bad' day? Or how can today be a replica of yesterday when we don't understand why yesterday went so well?
- How can our present work out if our past constantly undermines it? How can our future vision be achieved if our present problems remain unresolved?

One way to achieve harmony and consistency is to engage in a spot of time-travelling, one of the greatest gifts of our imagination. For example, we can revisit the last 24hrs and work systematically through them to build a detailed picture of, for example, the conversations we had and the actions we took, and use it to shape our day accordingly. Or we can travel into our desired future and, from there, look back at our present to ensure that our plans are consistent with us getting there.

As I have said, our Emotional Selves hate nothing more than being ignored or given unpersuasive answers, so being harmonious and consistent in answering them is critical. A few years ago, I came across this quote from American entrepreneur Jim Rohn that has stuck with me: "If you want to be taken seriously, be consistent." Well, here's my version: "If you want to take yourself seriously, be consistent."

Your transformation: on track, taking a diversion or off course entirely?

If I were to put you on the spot and ask you both questions, would your answers reassure or worry your Emotional Self? Remember, positive and helpful emotions are messages indicating our Emotional Selves are happy with us; difficult and unhelpful emotions mean the opposite. If you are feeling stressed, anxious, depressed or angry, the chances are that your Emotional Self is concerned either by your silence or your answers. As such, it will assume your transformation is, at best, on a diversion (hopefully short) or, at worst, off course entirely. So, now I will ask you to answer the questions using the box below.

Is today going to be like yesterday?	Is my past, present and future in harmony?

"My ambition was to work as a chef in the Far East, but my answers quickly exposed this as a fantasy. When I first contacted Mark, I was too anxious to even attend the morning meetings at my hotel where we discussed the days menus. My days were indistinguishable from each other, one bad day followed by another. As for my future aspirations, they were laughable. And yet, here I am, learning Japanese and immersing myself in Japanese cuisine. If all goes well, I'll be on a plane in the next six months."
Dylan

Helpful and unhelpful approaches to transformation

In my experience, many people fail to complete their transformational journeys not because doing so is beyond them but because they have what I call an 'unhelpful' approach to transformation. An unhelpful approach to transformation is characterised by specific ways of thinking, behaving, feeling and relating that undermine progress e.g., self-sabotage. Luckily, these ways are relatively easy to identify, which means creating a 'helpful' approach to transformation is similarly straightforward. All that is required is to work out the opposite of the ways someone is presently implementing e.g., instead of self-sabotage, someone would practice self-care. The two lists below include characteristics that I come across most often.

Again, the lists are not exhaustive, so feel free to add characteristics you think I have missed.

An unhelpful approach to transformation	A helpful approach to transformation
- impatience and the need for a 'quick fix'
- unrealistic goals and expectations
- perfectionism
- procrastination, avoidance
- self-sabotage
- self-criticism
- a lack of knowledge, information and resources
- poor knowledge, information and resources
- a lack of self-belief
- poor or unsustainable motivation
- too little or too much challenge
- the right goal but the wrong strategy
- not enough support or the wrong type
- difficult emotions such as stress, anxiety or depression
- unhelpful mindsets e.g., fear of failure, risk avoidant
- the wrong skills and abilities or the right ones that are poorly developed	- acceptance and a commitment to doing what it takes
- time and patience
- positivity – towards oneself and from others
- self-belief and trust in one's abilities
- turning setbacks into opportunities
- useful ideas, sound knowledge & effective resources
- the right skills and abilities, developed through practice and repetition
- alignment of realistic goals with effective strategies
- the right type of support and encouragement
- the right level of challenge
- positive emotions that help rather than hinder
- sustainable level of motivation
- a resilient mindset e.g., adversity is a great teacher, sensible risk-taking

In looking at each approach, do you instinctively connect with one more than the other? Or do you relate equally to both? Either way, it will be necessary for your successful transformation that you end up identifying with the helpful approach most or all of the time. To find out how near or far you are from achieving this, complete the following activity.

Taking each **helpful** characteristic, choose a number between 0 and 10 that captures how much of it you currently have. As a rule:

- scores of 7 or above indicate you are deficient or very deficient in a characteristic and will need to find more as a matter of urgency
- scores of 5 or 6 indicate you have some but not enough of a characteristic and that you will need to find more of it soon
- scores of 4 or below indicate you have enough or more than enough of a characteristic that you will need to strengthen or nurture.

What did you discover? Were your instincts regarding your existing approach to transformation confirmed or disproven? If you have an unhelpful approach, which helpful characteristics do you need more of, and how will you develop them? Might you need a Conversation With Impact to help? And now you know which approach you have been taking, does the current state of your transformation for good or for worse make more sense to you? I hope it does.

> "In all my years of failure at numerous personal and professional projects, it never occurred to me that my approach to transformation was the issue. If I am being honest, I never knew such a thing existed. Mark asked me to look at the table in his book and put a tick next to anything I recognised. There were a lot of ticks. That was a difficult day. It wasn't easy to accept that I had been steering my ship badly in the wrong direction. But that's behind me now."
> Chris

Imagined transformation is real transformation

When we start our journey of transformation or reach a crucial juncture on it, expectations of a positive outcome can be understandably high. This can make us vulnerable to what I call the 'evidence trap', an often unintentionally applied rule that states we need to see early or tangible change—depending on which stage we are at—to justify continuing on our journey. The most obvious example of the evidence trap is the failed New Year's Resolution e.g., "I need to lose two stones by March, or I am giving up." Timely evidence that our transformation is successfully underway can be a morale booster, but sometimes it is not forthcoming. How we respond determines whether we fall into the evidence trap or not.

In one particularly memorable therapy session, a client I was supporting shouted at me: "Transformation?! What transformation?!" In response, I asked him to take a leap of faith. "Just because you can't see it," I said, "doesn't mean it isn't happening." My client had come to see me for a crippling fear of being in enclosed spaces. So bad had his phobia become that he was finding driving and flying, which were vital for his work, increasingly complicated and traumatic. Entering my practice room, my client was well and truly 'trapped'. Everything he had tried to overcome his phobia had made little or no difference, so he had given up.

It is always a great feeling when as a practitioner, you can give people information that fundamentally changes what they know about their difficulties. What I could say to my client was that 'imagined' transformation is 'real' transformation. "At one level of consciousness, our mind/body systems do not distinguish between an imagined activity and a real one. When we visualise and rehearse overcoming our challenges in our imagination, we start laying down new neural pathways, like building foundations upon which to build a house. Then, when we come to do the activity for real, and our mind/body systems look for evidence that we have done it before, they are guided by what we have visualised and rehearsed."

This was how I pacified my client and gave him hope. "When you imagine yourself comfortably in enclosed spaces," I told him, "your mind/body system accepts this. Then, when you actually place yourself in these spaces, your mind/body system recognises what you are doing from your successful, imagined rehearsals. 'You've been here and done this before,' your system might say."

Over time, my client progressed through practice and repetition of imaginal and behavioural tasks. This combination of psychological approaches completes the formation of the neural pathways that underpin successful transformation—like when a finished house sits on top of its foundations. Ultimately, my client gained the evidence he needed to disprove the evidence trap rule: his imagined transformation was real. Our final session came after he returned from a holiday to California, which included a drive down the famous coastal road connecting San Francisco to San Diego. Like my client, too many people give up on their personal and professional transformation when they don't see early or timely evidence of progress, which is a genuine shame.

There is a caveat to imagined transformation is real transformation, however. The potentially unlimited abilities we have in our imaginations do not automatically transfer across into our reality (no matter what manifesting posts on Instagram and TikTok might claim). Anything we want to achieve has to be possible within the natural laws of the universe and our own capabilities. But this does not negate the validity of this powerful idea.

Focus on the process

The idea that imagined transformation is real transformation is an example of focusing on the 'process' of transformation and the outcome rather than just the latter. Why is this important? Outcomes can be highly seductive because they symbolise an end to our difficulties or the rewards of success, whereas processes—what we need to do to achieve outcomes—can represent effort and hard work. It can be easy to deceive ourselves into seeing process and outcome as the same thing when faced with the prospect of weeks or months of 'toiling' in process. This deception, a form of 'magical' thinking where someone expects an outcome, such as weight loss or career advancement, to happen without the necessary investment of time, energy and commitment, always ends in disappointment. This why concentrating on both is important.

I come across this form of magical thinking a lot in my work. To those who think like this, I offer my Ship's Rope and Mountain Climbing analogies, which I came up with to give people a reason to continue when the outcome feels impossible to achieve or seems too far away. By connecting process and outcome, the analogies succeed where magical thinking fails.

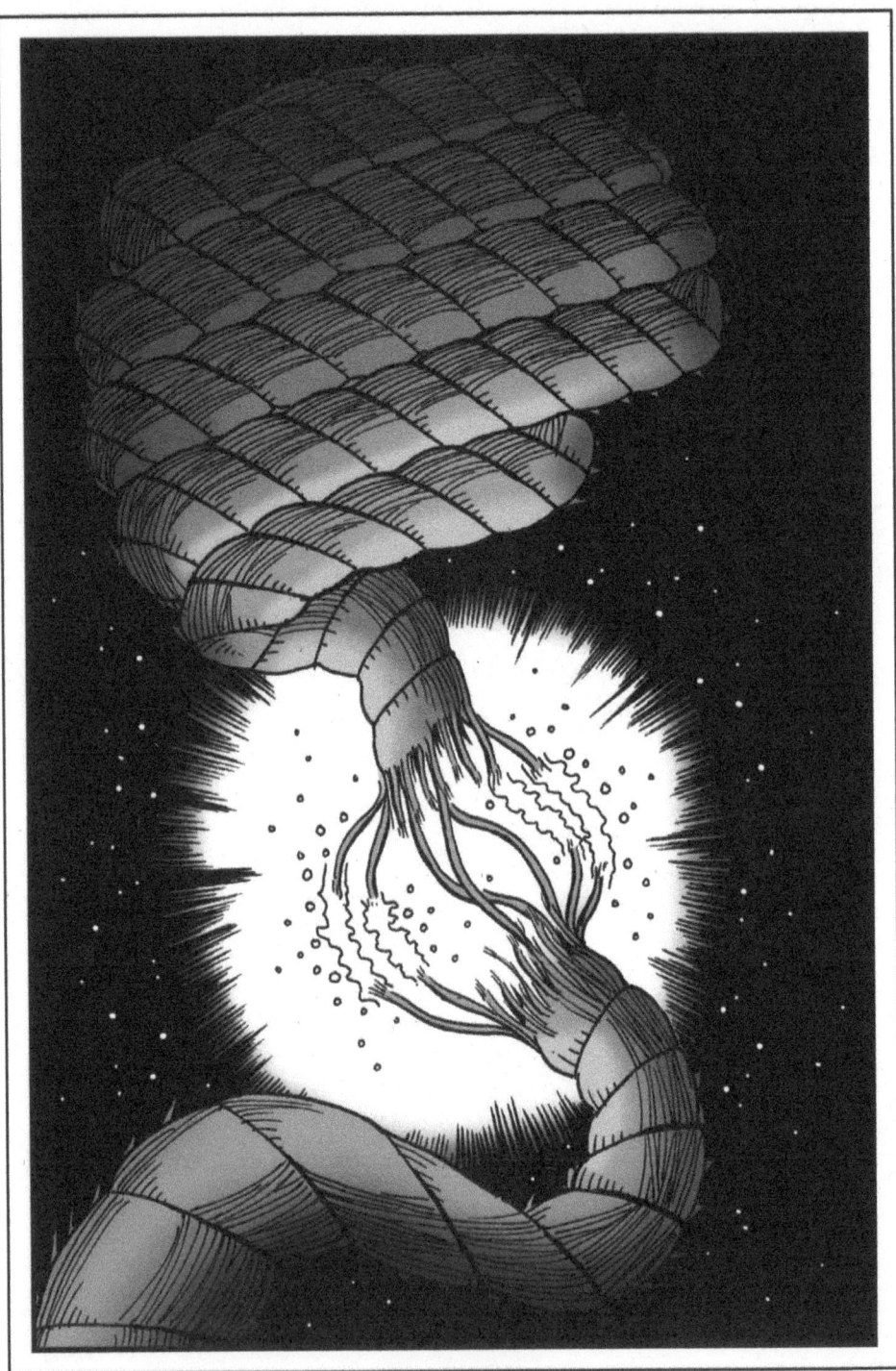

THE SHIP'S ROPE

The Ship's Rope

Imagine a thick piece of rigging or rope, the type used on large sailing ships. The rope represents the neural pathways in your mind/body system that contain and reinforce your difficulties. Now imagine starting your transformation and, as you do so, noticing the rope fraying a little as you put one foot in front of the other. You take a few more steps to check your eyes are not deceiving you, but they are not. The rope is fraying. However, a closer inspection reveals the rope is still thick and strong, and you decide that any further changes will only be surface level. You give the rope little thought for a time, and occasional glimpses confirm that it remains intact. However, as your journey progresses, the fraying becomes more apparent, and your attention switches once more to the rope. Your steps seem to be increasing the speed at which the rope is fraying, as does its weakness as it struggles to retain its strength. Encouraged, you quicken the pace of your transformation until, with a loud crack, the rope snaps. Your attention is drawn to fronds from the old rope flying magically through the air towards one another, combining as they do so. You realise that while the focus of your attention had been on the old piece coming apart, a new piece of rope made up of the escaping fronds had been forming in parallel. On close examination, it is just as robust. This new piece of rope symbolises the neural pathways in your mind/body that contain and will reinforce the foundations of your transformation.

Mountain Climbing

Firstly, I must add that my fascination with mountain climbing is inversely related to my ability to do it. The pursuit has, though, become valuable to me in my work, especially in its ability to convey a helpful approach to transformation.

- Before the climber leaves the ground, they undertake a great deal of preparation.

- Being unable to see the summit at the start of the climb due to cloud or bad weather does not necessarily stop the climber from beginning their ascent, and rarely, if ever, sees them cancel the climb completely.
- Once the climber has started, they make progress whether they can see the summit or not.
- While the climber has a planned route to follow, they accept it might have to change.
- Glances at the summit are permitted, but the climber's eyes never really leave the bit of rock in front of them.
- The climber accepts risks and setbacks as occupational hazards; falls are anticipated, but the climber knows their ropes will save them if they do fall.
- Ultimately, by getting all the above right, the climber knows they will reach the summit by climbing one small climb at a time.

Even as I write these bullet points, I am reminded how good mountain climbing is for capturing the critical relationship between process and content. So, if you ever feel demoralised at any point in your transformation, like the climber, remind yourself that a process is underway, with an outcome at its end. This way, you will avoid falling into the trap of thinking you never left the ground.

Stages of transformation

If we are to make our journey a success so we arrive at our destination, knowing and planning for the various stages of transformation we can travel through is vital for maximising progress and avoiding exhausting diversions. And we must also be aware of any fixed mindsets and challenge any unhelpful preconceptions about what stages lie ahead. So, are we:

- forgetting any key stages or, worse, ignoring known ones completely?

- Being too optimistic or too pessimistic, over or underconfident?
- Using past experiences, be they positive or negative, to shape our journey before it has even begun?
- Being realistic or unrealistic about what lies ahead?
- Over or underestimating our resources?

Fixed mindsets and unhelpful preconceptions are especially understandable. If we are plagued by self-doubt, they can make failure easier to accept, or if we see nothing but success ahead of us, they can make it simpler to blame external factors if we fail to achieve it. So, over the following pages, I suggest how you can avoid the above traps and make your journey as smooth and enjoyable as possible.

Early stages and a lesson in survival: Ray Mears

Our transformation can be fragile in its early stages when initial efforts can be subject to forces, such as self-doubt, seemingly intent on bringing them to a swift end. So, as we take our first tentative steps, we must focus equally on protecting them as we do on taking them. My 'Ray Mears' analogy is for these moments. When the risk of failure is high, a 'survival' instinct can be very handy. When I share this analogy with clients, they tell me it helps them to comprehend their situation and find the correct mindset.

(If you don't know who Ray Mears is, let me tell you. Ray is a survival expert of many decades, appearing in many television series. What he doesn't know about surviving in extreme climates isn't worth knowing.)

Ray sits in the middle of a Canadian forest, accompanied by an intrepid television documentary crew. All he has are the few provisions and resources an explorer can carry—and his wits. Civilisation lies hundreds of miles away. Around Ray rages an epic storm of wind, snow and sub-zero temperatures, conditions that can quickly kill a person. Ray gets to work on creating the warmth and shelter he needs to survive. Under cover of a tree, Ray takes two small sticks from his rusk sack and starts rubbing them together. After a few minutes, smoke appears as the friction from the sticks begins to generate heat, followed by a few sparks. Ray adds a small amount of dry woody material to the middle of this physical reaction, carefully protecting it with cupped hands and blows. A few seconds later, more smoke and then a tiny flame, as if by magic. Ray knows keeping this flame alive is critical and protects it from the raging storm as if his life depends on it—which it does. Over the next few minutes, Ray nurtures and grows the flame, adding increasing amounts of dry material until he eventually has a small fire going. Despite its fragility, Ray's shielding and steady feeding of the fire mean it has become self-sustaining, allowing him to step back and take stock. The camera crew turn their attention to the beauty of the wilderness surrounding them, taking the viewer on a panoramic tour of the surrounding forest that stretches as far as the eye can see. After a short while, the camera returns to Ray and there, unbelievably, is a roaring fire and a structure made of material Ray has foraged. There is still work to do, but Ray has the foundations in place.

Bigger visions, smaller visions

Journeys of transformation can stall or reverse, and destinations can fade or disappear if the bigger and smaller visions we have for them become out of sync. One client of mine illustrated this perfectly. Anthony came to see me for crippling anxiety and panic attacks, having left a 'safe' corporate career to set up his own business designing and building bespoke furniture. There was little doubt that Anthony and his business partner were highly talented. Their first clients were delighted by Anthony's ability to transform their visions into reality, leaving reviews on social media that sparked further interest. Anthony and his business partner had a big vision for their business. They saw clients enjoying their furniture worldwide, their lifestyles transformed by their 'works of art'. And yet, despite this big vision, Anthony sometimes never made it into his workshop, so severe had his anxiety and panic became.

It became clear that Anthony was not attending to the more mundane aspects—the smaller, day-to-day visions—of business. Bookkeeping, material costs, invoicing and time management were all neglected.

"I was in denial. If you don't look, it's amazing what you won't discover. My fantasy was that business could be endless days of creating beautiful furniture, with the boring stuff taking care of itself. So I got myself an accountant and a business advisor. It cost me money in the short-term, but it saved my business." Anthony

Once Anthony appreciated that the smaller visions of day-to-day business efficiency underpinned his bigger visions of global reach, critical success and delighted clients, his anxiety and panic disappeared.

Cave and Continuation Points

Cave and Continuation Points occur when the new life we are working hard to establish conflicts with the old one it is intended to replace. Cave and Continuation Points are sites of inner conflict and emotional turmoil when our past and future compete for control of our present. How we respond at our Cave and Continuation Points is crucial in determining if we 'cave' back into our old lifestyle or 'continue' into our new one. In these moments, we are reminded that a single burst of effort will not launch us into our new life but a series of them, often hard-fought and hard-won.

Cave and Continuation Points are characterised by distinct responses in how we:

- think
- behave
- feel
- relate.

It will come as no surprise that negative responses result in caving, positive ones in continuation. The New Year's Resolution is a perfect example of a journey of transformation littered with and threatened by Cave and Continuation Points.

Picture the scene. Someone comes out of the festive season determined to lose weight, get fit, change jobs or start a relationship. They make significant progress throughout January and maintain momentum during most of February. However, towards the end of February, signs appear that indicate trouble lies ahead. Snacks reappear in cupboards; gym visits are skipped; job searches tail off; relationship courage fades. By the middle of March, our once-determined soul has reached their Cave and Continuation Point, pushed and pulled by the competing forces of their old and new lives. How they think, behave, feel and relate determines what happens next.

"Mark walked me to my Cave and Continuation Point and asked me if I had ever been here before. I had, many times. Every

CAVE AND CONTINUATION

March, in fact! He got me to describe what usually happens using his think, behave, feel and relate approach. Saying it out loud, I realised how negative it was, how negative I was. The concept was so useful because it demonstrated why my annual attempts at personal and professional transformation always ended in disaster."

Lia

Lia discovered that her yearly caving happened not because this fate was inevitable but because she left her continuation to chance, not design. Once we had identified her negative thinking, behaving, feeling and relating and put together their positive counterparts, she made progress.

Sometimes the best way of understanding how we need to respond at our Cave and Continuation Points is to hear ourselves encouraging others, so if you were supporting a friend who has reached theirs, how would you encourage them? Would you:

- inspire them to believe in themselves and challenge negative thoughts? (thinking)
- point out how well they have done to get this far? (behaving)
- remind them of how their old life made them feel and how their new life could? (feeling)
- offer to support them or suggest they find someone else to, someone qualified perhaps? (relating)

I think you would.

I have, though, left the most important aspect to last. While the four types of responses available to us are critical, what turns them into ones that see us cave or continue is the emotional persuasiveness of our old life versus the new one we started our journey of transformation to establish. Whether it is losing weight or any other personal or professional ambition, continuing has to *matter* more—it has to be more emotionally persuasive. Unless and until we achieve this, we will always cave, a fate that no amount of thinking, behaving, feeling and relating will help us to avoid.

So at our Cave and Continuation Points, we have to ramp up the positives, amplify the benefits of our new life, and ensure that how we think, behave, feel and relate are consistent with achieving it.

"I sorted my responses and created a compelling emotional vision of my destination. This was the missing piece that my previous attempts had lacked." Lia

Divorcing the action from the emotion

As I have suggested over the last few pages, one of the most frustrating things about transformation can be the lack of an emotional 'reward' for our initial transformational efforts and how this can prompt us to give up. My 'Divorcing the action from the emotion' idea offers an explanation for this and why rewards are closer than we think.

When we seek to transform who we are, what we do and the life we lead, new actions still come, frustratingly, with old emotions. This is because our Emotional Selves who—remember are responsible for the emotions we experience—deliberately 'lag' behind us. Why they do might surprise you; it is to protect us. Emotional Selves want us to avoid the emotional lows that go with thinking we are making a success of our transformation when we are not. While reassured and excited by our decision to begin a journey of transformation, Emotional Selves also understand what it takes to see it through and the potential for early failure. So, to protect us, they keep us in our original emotional state until we present them with enough evidence that we can sustain our new actions. In this way, if we fail early on, we don't emotionally have far to fall. However, if we provide the evidence and stay on our journey, our Emotional Selves will willingly catch up and give us the emotional reward we deserve.

To summarise, Divorcing the action from the emotion happens in the following four stages:

- Stage One is when our Emotional Selves observe our new actions, appreciate that a journey of transformation is underway, but wait to see what unfolds.
- Stage Two is when our Emotional Selves become open to the idea of divorcing our new actions from old emotions as we present them with growing evidence of our transformation.
- Stage Three is when our Emotional Selves divorce our new actions from old emotions. because we have provided sufficient evidence. For a time, our new actions exist in an emotional limbo, attached to neither old emotions nor new ones.
- Stage Four is when our Emotional Selves fully catch up with us when they have worked out what new emotions to connect to our new actions.

Divorcing the action from the emotions is another example of connecting process and outcome. I hope it offers you a reason to continue in the absence of early emotional rewards.

Purposeful Drifting

I devised my Purposeful Drifting idea while working as a student coach and therapist in Higher Education. Every year, I would encounter two types of students: one that knew exactly what they wanted to do after graduation and one that didn't. The students who lacked a clear vision for their transformation after university were often understandably anxious, and I remember wanting to offer them a positive and helpful perspective with which to approach this next stage of their lives. It was to these students that I suggested Purposeful Drifting.

The idea was born out of my own experiences after leaving university. Although I spectacularly failed to appreciate it at the time, my own transformation into who I am now, both personally and professionally, was born in those days. I thought I was drifting aimlessly, but now I know better. Back then, I lived through periods of unemployment, self-destructive lifestyles and spells in jobs I was uniquely unqualified for, interspersed with genuinely positive and happy phases. I learnt so much about myself during those years after university, for good and sometimes for bad. Knowing I was 'purposefully drifting' and that everything I was accumulating would result in my personal and professional transformation would have made an enormous difference at the time. This was the message I wanted my students to take away.

All of us go through stages of transformation when we are uncertain about who we want to be, what we want to do and the life we want to lead. Purposeful Drifting enables us to appreciate these times. If we could tune into our self-talk as we drift with purpose, it might go something like this:

"I don't know where this journey is taking me or where it will end, but I am excited to find out."

Putting your transformation together

Below are the areas featured throughout this book that I have encouraged you to have conversations about with yourself and others; make sense of; identify patterns in; find acceptance in; set challenges for. Now you will get the opportunity to apply what you have learnt from this and the last five chapters to transform them, and ensure that you are on the right journey of transformation for your desired destination of transformation.

Internal transformation

- Mental and physical health and wellbeing.
- Thinking styles.
- Mindsets.
- Beliefs.
- Behaviours.
- Emotions.
- Identity, self-image.

- Self-esteem and self-worth.
- Self-confidence.
- Memories and past experiences.
- Past, present and future.

External transformation

- Yourself: identity, role and status.
- Home and family life.
- Relationships – personal and professional.
- Work, career and professional development.
- Health and wellbeing.
- Financial.
- Lifestyle.
- Social.
- Cultural.
- Environment.

The Transformation stage (and IMPACT Model generally) is designed to help you irrespective of how you are faring on your journey or how close you are to your destination. Over the following pages, you will get the chance to:

- identify the priority areas you want or need to transform
- create a story of transformation about your journey and destination
- generate ideas about your journey and destination if you have none, or develop existing ideas if you do
- time-travel to your future destination and go back through the journey that took you there.

Priority areas for transformation

Having come this far on your IMPACT journey, I hope you already have a good idea of the areas you wish to transform. However, don't worry if you don't as this next activity will help you to highlight your priority and non-priority areas. Why is this important? Aside from the more obvious need to avoid misdiagnosis, identifying and working on priority areas taps into an amazing piece of mind/body system functionality that I call the 'cascade effect'.

The cascade effect, in my language, is another way our Emotional Selves reward and encourage us. When they see that we know which priority areas to transform to ensure our thriving and surviving, Emotional Selves send us appropriate emotional messages in the form of feel-good emotions. Although these emotions relate directly to the priority areas we are transforming, they indirectly affect all others by 'cascading' down through them. Consequently, one or two things happen. Either these other areas require:

- less work because, in a more positive emotional state, we are better equipped to tackle them
- no work at all because it was only our negative emotional state that made them appear problematic.

So, over to you. Choose a number between 0 and 10 that highlights the internal and external areas on page 175 and 176 you need to transform as a matter of priority. As a general rule:

- scores of 7 or above indicate areas that you want or need to start working on immediately
- scores of 5 or 6 indicate areas that you want or need to work on once you have made sufficient progress in your 7+ areas
- scores of 4 or below indicate areas that require minor tweaks or that can be left alone entirely.

If you are still working things out, complete the activity as above, but use the 0–10 scale to capture degrees of certainty i.e., put 0 if you are sure an area isn't important, 10 if you think it is. Repeat the exercise until you have certainty.

What did you discover? For example, were your original suspicions confirmed, or were you surprised? What was the balance between internal and external areas?

Rewriting your story

Earlier in this chapter, I talked about the power of stories to kickstart our transformation, and this is where you get to write your story, but don't worry, I am not asking you to write War and Peace.

> "The beauty of Mark's task lay in its ability to drag from the depths of my unconscious a story I had written, but forgotten: one in which I believed in myself and my potential to make a success of my life."
>
> Sam

The first step is to read through the passage below; the second is to complete the table underneath. I have used the theatre as a metaphor for our mind/body system to convey the following. When our transformation is off-track, it can feel like we have lost control of our story and that the theatre itself – the building, stage, props, crew and actors working there – is deciding which one to put on. We have become part of the audience, a passive observer of our story, not its producer, director and scriptwriter. By rewriting your story, I hope you rediscover what was always true: the theatre—your mind/body system—doesn't choose the story; you do.

The theatre

Imagine you and I are sitting next to each other in a theatre. Sat high up in the gods, we have a good view of the stage. The play we have come to see is familiar because it is your life that is being told. The theatre is full, and there is the usual buzz ahead of the curtain going up. As the play commences, we look around to gauge the audience's reaction. Seeing faces of rapt attention, we give each other reassuring looks. However, a while into the play, we notice some shuffling in seats and whispered conversations—a general murmuring rippling through the audience. Then, unexpectedly, two people a few rows in front of us stand up and make for the aisle. The sudden movement attracts attention, and as if reading the minds of the departing couple, others start to follow them. What begins as a trickle turns into a flood of disappearing audience members. Startled, you grab someone and ask them why they are leaving. They reply that the play was no longer capturing their imagination. Someone else comments that the story had lost its direction. One-by-one, the audience exits the theatre until we are the only ones left; a night of hope and expectation turns into a disaster. We agree that drastic action is required to persuade audiences to return and send the actors home with the promise that we will contact them soon. I turn to you and exclaim that you have forgotten who you are.

"Who am I?" you shout back.

"You are the producer, director and scriptwriter," I say encouragingly, "but you have lost control of your own story."

"Will you help me rewrite it? Will you help me make it a success?" you ask.

I nod. We put our creative heads together, and a week later, we hand out a new script to our reassembled actors, who respond with energy and enthusiasm. A week later, the play reopens to great acclaim, and only after several standing ovations does the audience leave. You grab a group of friends talking enthusiastically about what they have just seen and ask them what they loved about the play.

"The main character, they transformed themselves," one of them says. "There was no hope in the old play, whereas this one was full of it."

Another audience member from the next row turns around and talks animatedly about the pivotal scene when the lead character broke free from what was holding them back. They add, with emotion, that they identified entirely with the main character. "I needed that tonight," they say.

You express your gratitude, and we sit back while an inspired audience leaves the theatre.

Your story

The table below allows you to reflect on your story so far and critically how you would like it to unfold. If you have existing ideas, then great, but if you need inspiration, look to your priority areas of transformation from the last activity. And if you have any go-to stories from novels, plays and films to draw from, make use of them too. Also, please take you time with this activity. Great stories, which yours can absolutely be, don't write themselves overnight.

Your story so far...	The plot twist: your story from now on...

T IS FOR TRANSFORMATION

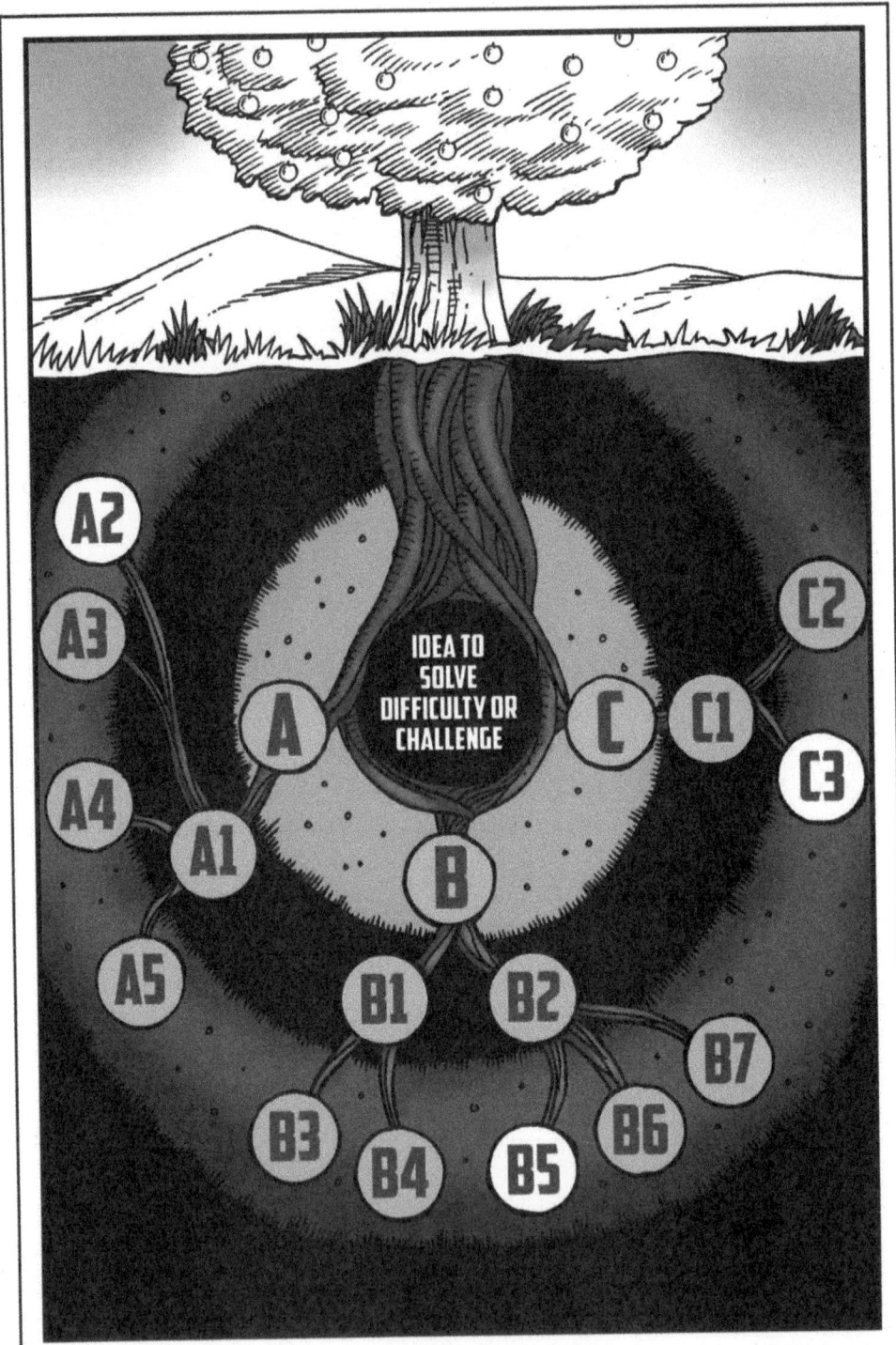

THE DARWINIAN TREE

T IS FOR TRANSFORMATION

Darwinian Tree

Sometimes it can be hard to generate the ideas we need to start our transformation and complete it. Nothing can be more elusive than a great idea or set of ideas, especially when we are struggling, which is why I came up with my Darwinian Tree activity. As the name suggests, the focus is on developing new or existing ideas and 'evolving' them into ones that can be acted upon. In my experience, great ideas are just below the surface, in our unconscious. They just need to be teased and coaxed out into our conscious awareness where they can be worked on.

To start, get a blank piece of paper or open a blank computer document and follow the steps below. Use the illustration as a guide to how your final Darwinian Tree might look.

- Step One: in the middle of the paper or document, write down the area you wish to transform e.g., your self-esteem, career or relationship. Use additional pieces or screens if you are working on more than one area.
- Step Two: spend a brief amount of time, no more than ten minutes, recording any ideas that come to mind, such as thoughts, observations or questions that seem to offer possible resolutions to the challenges you face in the area concerned. Note these down at the end of your first set of 'evolutionary' roots. You must write down anything that emerges, trusting your unconscious to offer you something valuable and relevant. At this stage, there needs to be an absence of judgement or questioning. Overthinking is the enemy here. The more time we wrestle with an idea, the easier it becomes to dismiss it as unworkable or unrealistic.
- Step Three: after a reasonable break—I recommend a day but go with what works for you—come back to your Darwinian Tree. At the end of your second set of evolutionary roots, note anything that arises from your first set of thoughts,

observations or questions. Again, limit yourself to no more than ten minutes.
- Step Four or more: repeat the above until at the end of one or more of your roots you have ideas that have evolved into ones you can act on.

What you are looking for by your final set of evolutionary roots are concrete ideas and details, such as those below. If you don't have this level of detail, then keep repeating the steps above. If, after several roots, an ideal fails to evolve into something tangible, then it can be safely discarded.

A successful Darwinian Tree will have:

- clear detailed visions
- goals and objectives, decisions, options or next steps
- names of people or organisations who can support you
- contact details, such as telephone numbers, email addresses etc.
- types of resources or equipment you will need
- names of helpful products and services
- times, dates and schedules
- techniques, strategies and plans.

This activity is close to my heart because it played a key role in my transformation a few years ago when I was struggling. Due to family separation, I had a lot of free time, which I found depressingly hard to fill. I initially noted a mixed bag of disconnected and seemingly pointless ideas, which I fought hard not to write off. However, I kept faith and set aside a piece of paper on which I had written:

- Indian food (I am a big fan)
- walking boots
- my father's name.

Over the next few days and weeks, this list evolved into:

- a ten-week beginners course in Indian cuisine run at a local Sixth Form
- joining a Peak District walking group that met regularly at weekends
- the establishment of my business, Conversations With Impact (my father ran his own business for many years)

I likened what my unconscious did that day to an old-fashioned juke box that selected three vinyl records it knew I wanted to listen to. Magic! I hope you find my Darwinian Tree activity as helpful and thought-provoking as I did, and that you now have an effective approach to idea generation.

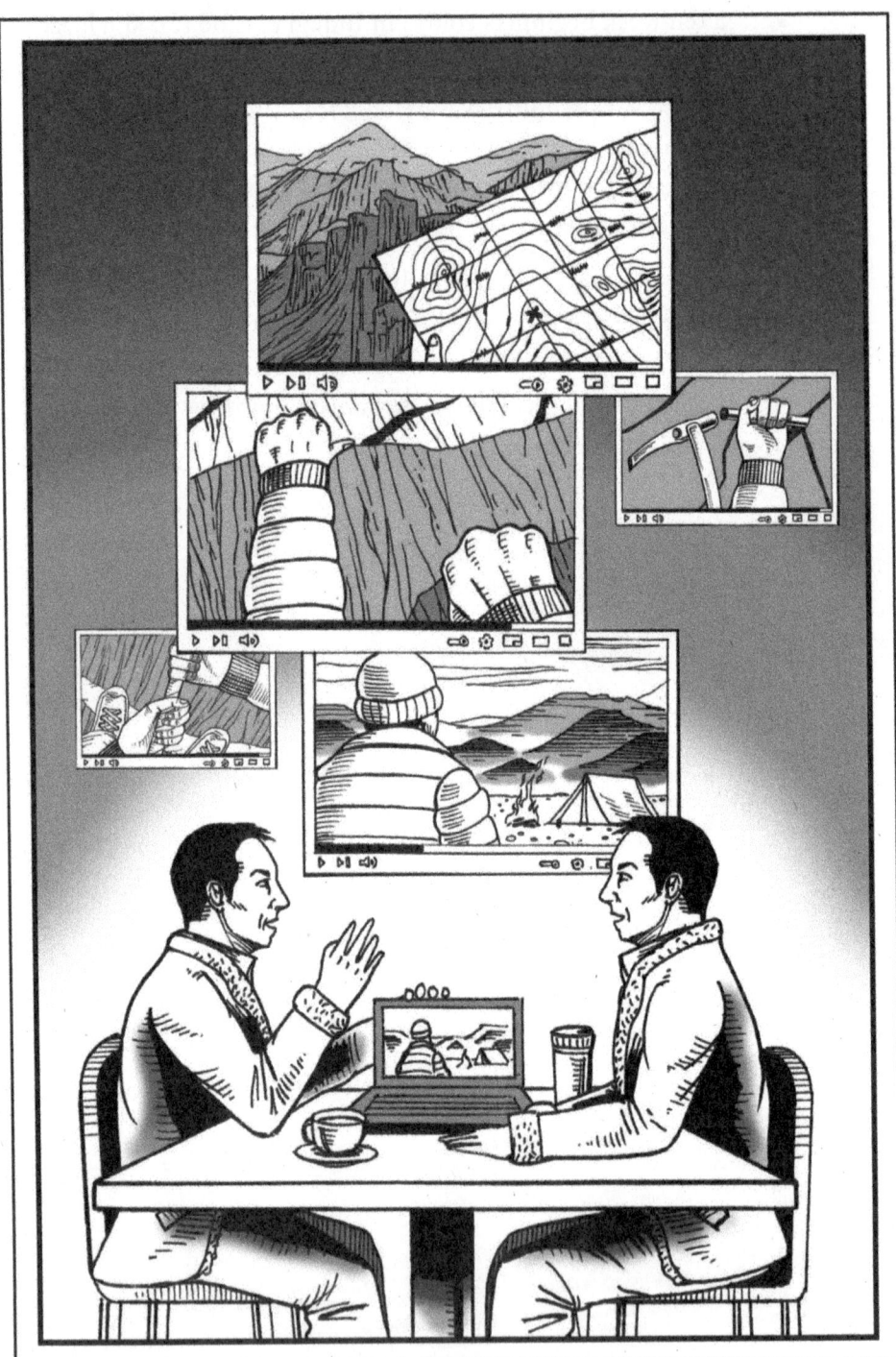

DESTINATION FINDER

The Destination Finder

"To know the road ahead, ask those coming back."
Chinese Proverb

One day, as you are sitting in a café near where you live, enjoying your favourite coffee, your future self enters the café and sits in the chair next to you. After a few minutes of small talk, your future self opens up a laptop and presses play on a video. On the screen, the video shows a place familiar to you, one you have visited many times in your imagination: your destination of transformation.

"Wow!" you exclaim. "I got there? I really got there?"

"Yes, you did," replies your future self.

After a short while, your future self plays a second video, a recording of your journey of transformation that ended when they entered the café you are in.

"Is that how you got, there? How I get there? To my future?" you ask.

"Yes," replied your future self, "that's the journey I've just completed and the one you're about to take."

My Destination Finder activity starts at your destination of transformation when you are who you want to be, doing what you want to be doing and living the life you want to be living. While it may seem odd to start at the end of your journey of transformation, not doing so would be a waste of your imagination's ability to time travel.

- In 'Attention and transformation', I talked about how our mind/body systems '...take the 'material' we gather and produce along the way and literally build our journey of transformation with it.' Imagine how much more—quality—material our mind/body systems would have to work with if we'd already made the journey several times. Travelling into and visualising our future is effectively handing our mind/body system a blueprint of the journey we want them to build.

- In 'Imagined transformation is real transformation', I discussed how 'At one level of consciousness, our mind/body systems do not distinguish between an imagined activity and a real one.' Similarly, if we are at our desired destination, our mind/body systems accept that we are there; and if we take a journey back through time from that destination to our present, it accepts this too. The result is that time travelling lays down neural pathways that contain our destination and the journey that took us there. I think this gives us a head start because reaching virtual destinations and completing virtual journeys makes the real ones easier to arrive at and complete.

My Destination Finder activity can help you visualise your desired destination and the journey to take you there. To start, look at the internal and external areas of transformation on pages 175 and 176 above and complete the steps below.

- Step One: establish your current reality: how is your life right now? Describe yourself, what you do, and the life you lead.
- Step Two: establish a desired future for yourself (your destination). Who would you like to be, what would you like to be doing, and what life would you like to be leading?
- Step Three: establish a timeline of when this transformation might occur, i.e., when you have reached your destination. Is it a month, six months or a year?
- Step Four: take some time to deepen the 'vision' of your destination. Make it a multisensory experience: imagine, engage and fully 'embody' this future state for yourself. Some questions you can ask are: What is happening? What do I see? Who am I now? What am I doing? What has changed? How have I changed? Speak as if your desired future were a reality, i.e., "This is who I am, this is what I am doing, and this is the life I am living."

- Step Five: from this future state, look back and describe the journey you took to get to your destination. Travel back through the stages you went through, speaking in the present as if you are there, e.g., "To get to this stage, I achieved this," or "To get to that stage, I achieved that."
- Step Six: bring yourself back to the present—the now—and explore what this exercise has given you in terms of learning, understanding and insight. What actions will you take to start the journey that will take you to your desired destination?
- Step Seven: approach this activity as a work in progress, regularly repeating it to ensure your progress is maintained

And finally: stories of transformation

I use stories in my work because if stories are about anything, it is transformation. So, I hope you enjoy the stories over the following few pages and that they inspire you to achieve the transformation you are after, along with my IMPACT Model.

Fast-flowing river

Imagine you are being swept along by a fast-flowing river. Try as you might, the current is too strong for you to swim to the riverbanks. Terrified and weak, you are at the mercy of the raging waters. Suddenly up ahead, you notice a tree that has been felled by a lightning strike, maybe from the same storm that caused your river to flood. A branch from the tree reaches out across the river.

You feel and hear a loud smack as your hands connect with and grip the branch. The water pushes against your waist and legs as before, but your new situation quickly sinks in; you are still in the fast-flowing river but no longer being swept along by it.

As your mind clears, two options present themselves. Drop back down into the river or shimmy along the branch? With a thud, you land on the riverbank, your knees bending to cushion your landing. In a state of shock and disbelief, you look down for reassurance. Your two feet, battered and bruised, are definitely connected to solid ground. You enjoy feeling connected to the riverbank for a few moments before asking yourself what to do next. Jump back into the river? Or climb up the riverbank? There is a definite pull from the river. After all, you were in it for a long time.

At the top of the riverbank, you look down over the other side. Several paths lead your gaze away into the distance. All look interesting to you, but one draws your attention. Checking in with your gut instinct, you choose the path directly ahead of you, feeling the movement of your body as you place one foot in front of the other, finding a nice rhythm. The noise of the river still penetrates your senses, but it dims with each step. And then you don't hear it at all.

The young man and the Buddha

A long time ago, in the East, lived a young man who, after suffering a run of bad luck, had slipped into such a state of despair that life didn't seem worth living. One night while drowning his sorrows in a bar, he overheard one customer telling a story to another about how the Buddha can work miracles for people and help them put their lives back together. Intrigued and prepared to give it one last shot, he set off to see the Buddha the following day.

On arrival at the Buddha's great palace, the young man begged for an audience. The Buddha was happy to see the young man, who told him the story he had heard and whether it was true—could he perform miracles and help him put his life back together? The Buddha confirmed the story's details and said he could help him. However, before they could start, the Buddha asked the young man to undertake some tasks he was too busy to do himself, promising to begin the miracles once they were completed.

The Buddha explained that the tasks involved visiting the homes of three people who lived nearby and who, incidentally, had also experienced misfortune in life. The young man was to bring back something from each of them. "What shall I bring back?" The young man asked.

"Oh, anything useful," replied the Buddha.

A little perplexed, the young man set off. The first person to be visited was a local farmer who the young man found working hard in a corn field. The farmer asked the young man why he had come. His visitor told him about his misfortune, meeting with the Buddha, and the need to return with a useful object. The farmer thought for a few moments and said, "I will give you something far more useful than a simple object—I will give you knowledge." And so he took his troubled guest and taught him how to sow, grow and harvest a field of corn until this knowledge was firmly planted in the young man's mind. Still a little confused, the young man nevertheless thanked the farmer. As he was about to leave, he remarked to the farmer that he no longer appeared to be suffering any misfortune. The farmer smiled and said he, too, had been to see the Buddha.

The next rendezvous was with an axe maker who, having enquired about the reason for the young man's visit, was regaled with the same story told to the farmer. The axe maker smiled knowingly, cast his gaze around his workshop and, seeing one of his finest axes, gave it to the young man. And then the young man did something he would never have thought possible only a week ago, he asked the axe maker how to make axes. "Show me how to do it so I can do it for myself," he asked.

Having acquired his second new skill, the young man prepared to leave. "And what of your misfortune the Buddha spoke about?" he asked the axe maker.

"Oh, that," reflected the craftsman, "that disappeared shortly after my trip to see the Buddha. Who do you need to see next, by the way?"

The young man replied that he must visit the saddle maker. "Does he live near here?"

"Not far," came the reply, "you're much closer than you might think." And so he set off to see the saddle maker, and when he found him, he discovered a similar story to those of the farmer and the axe maker. He left, of course, with a brand new saddle to add to his corn and axe—a saddle he had made himself.

The young man felt a little more upbeat at his second audience with the Buddha. He couldn't help feeling motivated by the three people he had just visited and the new knowledge and skills he had gained. *If they can overcome their misfortune, so can I*, he reflected. Indeed the Buddha commented on the apparent change in the young man's appearance—for the better. His young student agreed he felt more positive and explained that he had found his three tasks rewarding. But this newfound optimism was dented when the Buddha announced that the miracles would have to wait a while longer. "I must undertake an important journey," said the Buddha, "and set off at daybreak."

The young man could not hide his disappointment, but just as he felt despair begin to overwhelm him, his attention was distracted by a loud exclamation from the Buddha. "Ah!" said his illustrious teacher, "Now it is I who need your help."

"But how can I help you, of all people?!" exclaimed the young man. The Buddha explained that he was ill-prepared for his trip and needed certain supplies to make it possible: corn to make flour for his bread, an axe to chop wood for his fire and a good saddle for his horse. "I have none of these things," exclaimed the Buddha," and I can't make any of them either."

The young man suddenly felt a profound sense of calmness descend on him as he realised for the first time in a long time that he had something to offer. He proudly informed the Buddha that he could be of help to him and began throwing himself enthusiastically into his tasks. Soon after, he waved farewell to his wise mentor as he embarked on his journey.

It was some months before the Buddha was able to make good his side of the bargain. On his return, the Buddha thanked the young man for the corn, sturdy axe and comfortable saddle, as without these things, his trip would have been a disaster. Having shown interest in the Buddha's trip, the young man fell silent for a while as if lost in his thoughts. Seeing this distant look, the Buddha decided that now was the time to perform his miracle and began making preparations to do so. The Buddha's busyness shook the young man out of his peaceful trance, and stepping forward, he gently took hold of the Buddha's arm and told him not to bother as the miracles had already been performed.

Moving On

In an ancient land, a market stallholder plied his trade along a busy road joining two thriving cities. Each day he counted his blessings for having found such a lucrative site because the whole world, it seemed, travelled up and down that road as they went about whatever was their business. In the middle of their journeys, the travellers got tired and hungry, craving rest and refreshment, needs our market stall holder was happy to provide for. As the money rolled in and he became wealthy, he became determined to stay rooted to that spot. Nothing and nobody he promised himself would persuade him to let go of his pitch and move on.

However, as is the way of the world, times changed. New towns and cities sprung up across the land, drawing people and traffic away from the road. And as is another way of the world, there are those who understand the inevitability of change and the need to go with it and those who don't. Our market stallholder was one of those who didn't. "Why should I let go and move on?" he would say defensively to his dwindling band of customers, "Business will pick up!"

Convinced by his own arguments, he had too much personal investment in staying put. He developed business strategies to attract people back to the area, investing more of his money and himself and becoming more determined to stay put even as those around him were packing up.

One particular day, an awful day in fact for our market stall holder as business was especially poor, a man approached on a horse and dismounted in front of the stall. Our trader noted that his horse was a fine one, as were his clothes which were clearly made of the finest cloth. But aside from his finery, something else caught the eye of our trader: it was the man's look—untroubled, tranquil, at peace with the world. Peering into the stall, the stranger saw a dejected figure. Glancing around, he saw precious few reasons for this miserable tradesman to be here. Engaging him in conversation, the stranger asked how he had arrived at this particular spot. In reply and touched that someone was taking an interest in him, our trader recounted how he had spotted the opportunity to set up and start trading. He had foreseen that the road would attract more and more people because the two cities it connected were growing. His previous business wasn't going anywhere, he continued, and letting that go and moving on seemed the natural thing to do. Much to his surprise, the hero of our story repeated these words quietly to himself— "the natural thing to do." Both men sensed the meaning of the moment. In the few seconds of silence that passed between them were born the first stirrings of possibility.

Dropping some pennies into the trader's hands, the nameless rider thanked him for his hospitality and rode on. The market stallholder combined the pennies with his meagre takings and began closing down for the day. He loosened his stall's ropes and lifted the poles they were attached to out of the ground. Anyone noticing him would have seen him go about his business more freely, the words 'letting go and moving on' circling in his imagination like the magnificent birds of prey gliding high above on warm currents of air.

As the sun rose the next day, no market stall could be seen.

Summary of Chapter Six

- Transformation is both the journey and the destination.
- Transformation can be understood in terms of who, what, where, when, why and how.
- There is a close relationship between where we focus our attention and how our transformation unfolds.
- Transformation involves travelling through time and visiting our past, present and future.
- There are helpful and unhelpful approaches to transformation.
- Imagined transformation is real transformation.
- There are different stages of transformation.
- Transformation can be achieved in many ways, such as through storytelling and the patient evolution of ideas.
- Stories are a great source of inspiration.

MARK EVANS

A Final Thought

I hope reaching the end of my book marks the start of your journey of transformation. Please keep returning to the book, the model and its six stages. Like a good story, it can give you something new each time, enabling you to be who you want to be, do what you want to be doing and live the life you want to lead. As you look ahead, remember to:

- change your conversations into Conversations With IMPACT
- make sense of why things are as they are and find MEANING
- step back from your PATTERNS to identify and replace those that aren't helping with those that will
- believe in yourself as someone with potential, and close any Fantasy-Reality Gaps through ACCEPTANCE
- make CHALLENGE work for you, not against you, by following The Goldilocks Principle: not too little, not too much, but just right
- learn the art of TRANSFORMATION to enjoy the journey and arrive at your destination.

www.conversationswithimpact.co.uk

MARK EVANS